BIBLE TREASURY

FOR LDS CHILDREN

BIBLE TREASURY

FOR LDS CHILDREN

Written by Sherrie Johnson
Illustrated by Jerry Harston and
Leslie Harston

DESERET BOOK COMPANY, SALT LAKE CITY, UTAH

Library of Congress Cataloging-in-Publication Data

Johnson, Sherrie.
   Bible treasury for LDS children / text by Sherrie Johnson ; art by
Jerry Harston.
     p.   cm.
   Summary: A collection of over sixty Bible stories from the Old and
New Testaments, from Creation to the travels of Paul.
   ISBN 1-57345-162-2
   1. Mormon children Prayer-books and devotions—English. 2. Bible
stories, English. [1. Bible stories.] I. Harston, Jerry, ill.
II. Title.
BX8643.C56J64   1999
220.9'505—dc21   99-39719
                                                    CIP

Printed in the United States of America   42316-6194
10 9 8 7 6 5 4 3 2 1

To Douglas, Julie, Ian, Shad, Joseph, Michaelia, and Mhari Mills
with much love

Contents

BIBLE TREASURY

FOR LDS CHILDREN

Long before we were born, we lived in heaven with our heavenly parents.

Heavenly Father held a meeting with all of us. At this council in heaven, Heavenly Father told us about his plan of salvation.

Heavenly Father said, "I will make an earth for you to live on. While you are there, I will give you commandments. This will be a test. If you obey all my commandments, you will pass the test. Then you can come back to live with me again. I will give you everything I have. We will be happy together forever.

"But if you sin—or disobey my commandments—you cannot come back to live with me. This test will be hard, but I will help you."

Heavenly Father told us more about his plan. He said, "Now, I know that you might sin. But I love you, and I want you to come back to live with me. So I will send a Savior to the earth. If you have faith in him and repent, he will suffer the punishment for your sins. To have faith means to trust him and believe him. It means to follow and obey him. If you will do this, you will be able to come back and live with me again. This is the plan of salvation."

We thought this was a good plan. We thought it was so good, we shouted for joy.

Heavenly Father asked, "Whom shall I send to be the Savior?"

We had a brother in heaven named Jehovah. He was the first of Heavenly Father's spirit children. We knew he loved us.

Jehovah said, "Here am I, send me." He said he would show us the way. Then we could decide if we wanted to follow him and be saved. He would not force us to do anything.

Jehovah loved Heavenly Father. He said to Heavenly Father, "This is your plan. So I will give the glory and honor to you."

We also had a brother named Lucifer. Lucifer stepped forward too. "Here am I, send me," Lucifer said. "I will save everyone. I will make them obey me. And since I will save them, give me the glory and honor."

After listening to Jehovah and Lucifer, Heavenly Father said, "I will send the first."

Lucifer became very angry. He tried to persuade everyone to follow him instead of Jehovah.

Many of our brothers and sisters in heaven followed Lucifer. Together they fought against Heavenly Father and the rest of the spirit children. But finally, Heavenly Father cast Lucifer and his followers out of heaven. This meant they would never be born on the earth or have bodies. They would never be able to go back to Heavenly Father or become like him.

With Lucifer gone, those of us who chose to follow Heavenly Father and Jehovah waited our turn to be born on the earth. When our time came, our spirits entered bodies and we were born to a mother and father on earth. We are here now to be tested, so that we can become holy like our Heavenly Father.

Jehovah waited for his turn on earth, too. When he lived on the earth, his name was Jesus. He also has many other names. Sometimes we call him Lord or Savior.

—

ABRAHAM 3

Heavenly Father asked Jehovah to make an earth for us to live on. He told Jehovah how to create the earth, and Jehovah obeyed.

First, Jehovah divided the light from the darkness. He called the light day and the darkness night. When he finished, he called that time the first day.

Next Jehovah made the sky over the earth. He divided the waters above the sky from the waters under the sky. When he finished, he called that time the second day.

Jehovah separated the waters below the sky from the dry land. He called the land earth and the waters seas. He commanded the earth to bring forth grass, seed, and fruit. When he finished, he called that time the third day.

Next Jehovah placed lights in the sky. He made stars and a moon to rule the night. He also made the sun to rule the day and give light to the earth. When he finished, he called that time the fourth day.

Jehovah next made fish to swim in the seas and birds to fly in the air. When he finished, he called that time the fifth day.

Jehovah put animals and insects and worms on the earth. Then Heavenly Father said, "Now let us make man in our image. Let them rule over the fish of the sea, over the fowl of the air, over the cattle, and over all the earth."

So Heavenly Father and Jehovah created man in their image, male and female. They named the man Adam, and Adam named the woman Eve.

Heavenly Father put Adam and Eve in a beautiful garden called Eden. The Garden of Eden was a paradise where there was no sickness or death. Nothing grew old or ugly. There were no thorns or weeds and no sadness.

When God placed Adam and Eve in the Garden of Eden, he commanded them to take care of it. Then he said, "You may eat anything in the garden, except fruit from the tree of knowledge of good and evil."

When Adam and Eve were settled in Eden, Heavenly Father said, "It is good," and he called that time the sixth day.

Then Heavenly Father and Jehovah rested. This time of rest was the seventh day. Because of this, Heavenly Father made the seventh day of every week holy. He called it the Sabbath.

—

GENESIS 1–2; MOSES 2–3;
ABRAHAM 4–5

For a time Adam and Eve lived peacefully in the Garden of Eden with the animals. They were naked, but they were not embarrassed. Lucifer was also there. He was now called Satan.

Satan wanted to destroy God's plan of salvation. He put it into the heart of a serpent to tempt Eve.

The serpent asked Eve, "Has God told you not to eat the fruit from every tree in the garden?"

Eve answered, "We may eat the fruit of all the trees except the tree of knowledge of good and evil. God told us not to eat that fruit. He said that if we ate that fruit we would surely die."

"You shall not surely die!" the serpent lied. "If you eat that fruit, your eyes shall be opened. You shall be like gods, knowing good and evil."

Eve began to want the fruit. It was pretty. It would taste good. But most of all, it would make her wise. Finally she ate the forbidden fruit. Then she took some to Adam, and he also ate.

Now their eyes were opened, and they saw that they were naked. They were embarrassed, so they sewed fig leaves together to make aprons to cover themselves.

5

Later, during the cool of the day, Adam and Eve heard the voice of God calling them. They knew they had disobeyed Heavenly Father, and they were ashamed to face him. Quickly they hid themselves.

Heavenly Father called, "Where are you?"

"I heard your voice," Adam answered, "and I was afraid, because I was naked. So I hid."

God asked Adam, "Who told you that you were naked? Have you eaten the fruit I commanded you not to eat?"

Adam said, "The woman gave me the fruit, and I ate it."

Then God asked Eve, "What have you done?"

Eve answered, "The serpent tricked me, and I ate the fruit."

Heavenly Father said to the serpent, "Because you have done this, you are cursed more than all other beasts. You shall crawl upon your belly and eat dust all of your life. One of the woman's seed, Jesus Christ, shall bruise your head, and you shall bruise his heel."

Then Heavenly Father told Eve, "In sorrow you will bring forth children. Your desire will be to your husband, and he will rule over you."

Finally Heavenly Father spoke to Adam: "The ground shall be cursed for you. In sorrow you shall eat from it all of your life. By the sweat of your face you will eat your bread."

Then Heavenly Father said to Jehovah, "The man now knows good and evil. Send him out of the Garden of Eden so that he cannot eat the fruit of the tree of life and live forever. Also, place cherubim and a flaming sword to guard the way of the tree of life."

And so Adam and Eve were cast out of the Garden of Eden into a strange new place. This new world had thorns and weeds. In it, Adam and Eve would experience sickness, sorrow, pain, and many other things that were not in the Garden of Eden. But they would also experience wonderful things like love and joy.

Together Adam and Eve began to grow plants for food and to keep cattle and sheep. Their days were long and hard now. But they prayed and worshipped the Lord and they heard his voice speaking to them from the Garden of Eden. He told them what to do to return to him.

One commandment the Lord gave Adam was to offer sacrifice. To do this, Adam piled stones to make an altar. He put wood on the altar to make a fire. Then he killed a lamb and put it on the fire. Adam did not understand why the Lord wanted him to sacrifice lambs, but he obeyed the Lord anyway.

One day while Adam was sacrificing a lamb, an angel came to him. The angel asked Adam, "Why do you sacrifice to the Lord?"

"I don't know why," Adam answered. "I only know the Lord commanded me to do it."

Then the angel explained, "When you sacrifice a lamb, it is a symbol of the sacrifice of Jesus Christ. Many years from now, Jesus Christ will be sacrificed to pay for the sins of all mankind. Jesus will suffer the punishment for your sins, if you repent of them and have faith in him. For this reason, you must pray to God in the name of Jesus Christ. And you must repent of your sins."

After this, Adam and Eve were taught the gospel and were baptized.

—

GENESIS 2–3; MOSES 4–5; 6:48–68

THE FIRST MURDER

Adam and Eve loved Heavenly Father very much. Therefore, they taught their children the gospel.

But Satan told the children, "Believe it not!" Some of the children did not believe. They loved Satan more than God. They became very selfish. They began to sin and would not repent.

Adam and Eve had two more sons.

They named the first son Cain. Eve was very happy when Cain was born. She said, "I have got a son from the Lord. Surely he will love the Lord."

But Cain would not listen to his parents. He chose to follow Satan instead of the Lord.

The second son was named Abel. He loved the Lord and tried to obey all his commandments.

When Cain grew up, he became a farmer. When Abel grew up, he kept sheep.

THE FIRST MURDER

Because he loved the Lord, Abel sacrificed a lamb from his flock of sheep. The Lord accepted Abel's sacrifice.

Satan told Cain to sacrifice some of the fruits and vegetables he had grown, and Cain did so. But the Lord had not said to sacrifice fruits and vegetables. He had said to sacrifice lambs. Besides that, Cain made his sacrifice out of love for Satan, not love for the Lord. And so the Lord could not accept Cain's sacrifice. Cain became very angry.

The Lord said to Cain, "Why are you angry? If you obey me, I will accept you."

But Cain would not follow the Lord. He chose to follow Satan. As the days passed, he became more greedy and selfish. The fruits and vegetables he grew were no longer enough for him. He also wanted Abel's sheep. Satan said to him, "If you kill your brother, you can have his sheep."

One day Cain went into the field to talk with Abel. As they spoke, Cain became angry. He sprang at his brother and killed him. Then he hurried away from the field and pretended he didn't know what had happened.

The Lord asked Cain, "Where is your brother Abel?"

Cain said, "I don't know. Am I my brother's keeper?"

Then the Lord said to Cain, "Your brother's blood cries out to me from the ground. Now you are cursed. Your fields will no longer grow fruits and vegetables for you, and you will wander the earth without a home."

With that curse upon him, Cain left and lived in the land of Nod, on the east of Eden.

Adam and Eve were filled with grief. They wanted a child who would love the Lord and obey his commandments. They prayed, and the Lord blessed them with a son named Seth. Like Abel, Seth loved the Lord and obeyed his commandments. Because of this, he was worthy to receive the priesthood from his father, Adam. The priesthood was passed down from father to son through all the generations.

—

GENESIS 4; MOSES 5–6

While a young man named Enoch was traveling, he heard a voice from heaven speak to him. The voice said, "Enoch, my son, prophesy to this people. Tell them to repent! Tell them I am angry with them because their hearts have become so hard."

Enoch knew it was the Lord speaking to him. He bowed down to the ground and said, "I am so young! And the people dislike me because I don't speak well. Why am I chosen to be your servant?"

The Lord answered, "Go and do as I have commanded you. No one will hurt you. Open your mouth to speak, and I will give you the words."

Then the Lord said, "Anoint your eyes with clay, and wash them, and you shall see."

Enoch obeyed. As he washed away the clay, he saw a marvelous vision. He saw all of God's children, and he saw many other wonderful things that people can't see with their natural eyes. When he told people what he had seen, they said, "The Lord has sent a seer to his people."

After that, Enoch began to prophesy and tell the people to repent. He told them that to be happy they must follow God. Many people repented of their sins. But many others were offended. They made excuses, refused to listen, and spoke against Enoch. But no man dared to hurt Enoch. Even those who refused to obey knew that Enoch walked with God.

One man named Mahijah said to Enoch, "Tell us plainly who you are, and where you came from."

Enoch answered, "I came from the land of Canaan. My father taught me in all the ways of God. One day as I traveled by the sea, I saw a vision. In the vision, I saw heaven, and the Lord spoke to me. To keep his commandment, I speak these words to you. It was the God of heaven who spoke to me. He is my God and your God. Why do you deny him?"

As Enoch bore his testimony, the people trembled.

Enoch said more: "Satan has come among men and tells them to worship him. Men follow him and become carnal, sensual, and devilish. Because of this, they are shut out from the presence of God unless they repent."

Many people believed Enoch's words and wanted to be baptized and join the Church. After they were baptized, they lived together in peace. They grew in faith and love for one another and for Heavenly Father.

The people who did not believe Enoch's words became even more angry. They didn't want people to join the Church. They gathered together to fight against the believers. But Enoch had so much faith that when he commanded, the earth shook and the mountains moved. When the people saw this, they feared Enoch and his people so much that they stopped trying to fight against them.

Left alone, Enoch and his people lived together in peace and love. They made sure that no one was ever hungry or poor. They were always kind, and they obeyed every commandment God gave them. Thus they became so righteous that the Lord came and stayed with them.

He blessed the land and called it and the people Zion because they were pure in heart.

Finally, because they were so righteous, God took them and their city up into heaven. From then until the time of the Flood, any person who loved God and obeyed his commandments as Enoch had was taken up to join the people of Zion. The wicked who did not repent stayed on the earth.

One day, Enoch saw these wicked people in a vision. He also saw the Lord looking at these people and weeping.

"How is it you can weep, since you are holy?" Enoch asked.

The Lord answered, "These are my children. I commanded them to love one another and to choose me, but they do not love each other. They love Satan. For this reason, they shall die in the floods. After they die, they will be in spirit prison. There they will suffer torment until Jesus suffers for their sins and they repent. This is why I weep."

When Enoch understood these things, he was filled with so much sorrow that he also began to weep for his brothers and sisters who would not repent and be saved.

—

MOSES 6–7

NOAH AND THE GREAT FLOOD

Noah was a just man who loved God. For 120 years he tried to teach the gospel to the people who lived on the earth. He warned them, "Repent of your sins and be baptized in the name of Jesus Christ, and you shall receive the Holy Ghost. If you do not do this, the floods will come."

But the people were violent and full of anger and wickedness. They wouldn't listen to Noah.

Finally, God told Noah to build a great ship

called an ark. He told Noah to build it out of gopher wood. It was to be 450 feet long, 76 feet wide, and 45 feet tall.

Noah went to work and built the ark. When he had finished, God told him exactly what to put inside it. Of all the clean beasts, he told Noah to take seven males and seven females. Of the unclean beasts, he told Noah to take two males and two females. He told Noah to put food in the ark for all the animals and for his family, and seeds to plant after the Flood. Noah did all that Heavenly Father commanded. Then Noah, his wife, his sons—who were named Shem, Ham, and Japheth—and his sons' wives all moved into the ark.

It began to rain. It rained for forty days and forty nights. The water covered the ground and then the houses and the trees. Then it covered the mountains. The people who had scoffed at Noah and refused to repent were drowned.

After the rains stopped, Noah and his family floated on the great sea while the water slowly went down. After 150 days, the ark finally came to rest on the mountain of Ararat. Noah waited forty more days. Then he opened a window and sent out a dove. The dove could find no place to land, and it came b

After seven more days, Noah again sent out the dove. It returned again, but this time it had an olive leaf in its mouth. The sight of the leaf filled Noah and his family with hope.

Noah waited seven more days, then sent the dove out again. This time it never returned. It had found a place to live! After more than a year, the day finally came when Noah opened the door and his family and the animals left the ark.

To thank God for being saved, Noah built an altar and offered sacrifices. In return, God made a promise to Noah. This promise is called a covenant. God said, "The waters shall never again come to destroy all living things. As a token of this promise, I will place a rainbow in the sky."

After leaving the ark, Noah farmed the earth and made a home for his family. Children were born, and the earth was filled again with living things.

—

GENESIS 6–9;
JOSEPH SMITH TRANSLATION (JST)
GENESIS 8; MOSES 8

Many years after the Great Flood, cities and towns again filled the earth. The people all spoke the same language and could understand one another.

Just as before the Flood, most of the people did not love the Lord. All they cared about were fine clothes, fancy houses, and jewelry. They became very wicked.

In the city of Babel, the people were so wicked and foolish they decided to build a tower tall enough to reach heaven and find God. Soon hundreds of workers were busy building the tower. But this displeased the Lord very much. He said, "We will change their language so they cannot understand one another." And it was done.

Now, instead of one language, there were many. When a man asked his friend for tools, the friend could not understand what he said. There was confusion everywhere. No one knew what to do. They separated into groups that understood the same language, and the building stopped.

One man named Jared wanted his family and friends to stay together. He asked his brother, Mahonri Moriancumer, to pray and ask the Lord to let them keep the same language.

When Mahonri Moriancumer prayed, the Lord answered his prayer. He let Jared and his family keep their language. He also told them to build eight boats, called barges. The brother of Jared was to use the barges to take his people to a new land. There they would be free to worship the Lord. The brother of Jared and his people obeyed. They built the barges and sailed to the promised land. These people were called the Jaredites. The land they went to is now called America.

—

GENESIS 11; ETHER 1–3, 6;
JUVENILE INSTRUCTOR 1 MAY 1892, 282

In the land of Ur there lived a young man named Abram. His father, Terah, worshipped idols, but Abram worshipped the Lord. He wanted the peace and happiness that are blessings of the priesthood.

Abram told Terah that he should worship the Lord instead of idols. But Terah did not listen. Instead he gave Abram to false priests to be sacrificed.

The false priests tied Abram's hands and feet and laid him on their altar. One of the priests raised a knife to kill him. But Abram had much faith, and he cried to the Lord for help. Suddenly an angel appeared to untie Abram. The priest fell dead, and the altar and all the idols

broke into pieces. "I have come to free you and to take you away from your father's house to a land you do not know," the angel said. "I will lead you by my hand, and I will give you my priesthood."

When the time came for Abram to leave Ur, he took his wife, Sarai, his nephew, Lot, and Lot's family with him. Following the Lord's command, they went north to the land of Haran.

When Abram was seventy-five years old, there was a great famine in Haran. Once more the Lord spoke to Abram: "Arise, and take Lot with you out of the land of Haran. I am the Lord your God, and I will keep you safe. From this time, everyone who accepts the gospel will

belong to your family and will receive the priesthood. Through the priesthood, all the families of the earth will be blessed."

Abram obeyed the Lord. He took his family and Lot's and journeyed to the land of Canaan. Dwelling in tents, the family made their way south, stopping often to build an altar and worship the Lord. When they finally reached Canaan, the Lord appeared to Abram and said, "Unto your seed will I give this land." But

famine was also in the land of Canaan, so Abram did not stay but traveled on to Egypt.

In Egypt, Abram's flocks and herds grew until he had hundreds of animals. He also earned much silver and gold and hired many servants. By the time the famine was over, Abram was a very wealthy man.

—

ABRAHAM 1–2;
GENESIS 11–13

ABRAHAM'S TEST OF FAITH

Abram and Sarai were old now and had never had a child.

One day the Lord said to Abram, "Fear not, Abram. I am your shield and your reward."

Abram replied, "Yes, but I have no children."

The Lord said, "You shall have a son, and he will have children, and his children will have children. Look at the sky and count the stars. That is how many descendants you will have."

Abram believed the Lord, but year after year

passed, and still he and Sarai had no children. Sarai knew that she was getting too old to have children. She took her maid, Hagar, to Abram and said, "Let Hagar be your wife and give us a child." So Abram married Hagar, and when he was eighty-six years old, Hagar had a baby boy. They named the baby Ishmael, which means "God hears."

When Abram was ninety-nine years old, the Lord came to him again and said, "Your name shall no longer be Abram. Your name shall be

Abraham, for I will make you a father of many nations. Your wife Sarai shall be called Sarah. I will bless her and give you a son from her also. She shall be a mother of nations."

When Abraham heard these words, he fell upon his face and rejoiced. He knew that Sarah was too old to have children. The son the Lord promised him would be a miracle.

Finally, when Sarah was ninety-one years old, she had a son. She named him Isaac, which means "laughter." She explained, "God has made me laugh with joy, and everyone who hears what has happened will laugh with me."

Isaac grew up to be a fine young man who loved the Lord and wanted to obey him. One day the Lord said to Abraham, "Take your son Isaac, whom you love, and go to the land of Moriah. There you shall sacrifice Isaac."

Abraham must have been troubled by this command. How could he sacrifice the son he loved so much? But he had great faith in the Lord. Early the next morning, he arose and saddled a donkey. He took Isaac, two servants, and wood for the sacrifice. They traveled three days to reach the mountain of Moriah.

When they arrived, Abraham said to his servants, "Stay here with the donkey while Isaac and I go up the mountain to worship."

Then Abraham laid the wood on Isaac's back, took a knife and a torch to make the fire, and started up the mountain.

Isaac asked, "Where is the lamb for a burnt offering?"

Abraham answered, "My son, God will provide a lamb."

When they reached the place for the sacrifice, Abraham built an altar, bound Isaac, and laid him on the wood. But as he took the knife to kill his son, a voice stopped him.

"Abraham, Abraham!"

Abraham answered, "Here I am."

"Do not touch the young man," the voice from heaven said. "Now I know that you love God."

As Abraham looked up, he saw a ram caught in the bushes by its horns. With great joy, he gave the ram as a burnt offering. Then, with grateful hearts and filled with the peace that comes from being faithful, Abraham and Isaac found the servants and returned home.

—

GENESIS 16–17, 21–22

When Sarah died, Abraham was very old, but Isaac was not yet married. This worried Abraham. The women who lived in the land of Canaan worshipped idols and did not believe in God. Where could Isaac find a righteous wife?

Abraham called his servant Eliezer to him and said, "Go to my relatives in Haran and find a wife for my son Isaac."

Eliezer took ten camels loaded with presents and traveled for many days to the land of Haran. As he neared the city, he stopped at a well. Unsure what to do next, he prayed.

"Oh, Lord God," Eliezer said, "I stand by the well, and the daughters of the city come out to draw water. I will ask the women to give me a drink. Let the woman you have chosen to be Isaac's wife answer me by saying, 'Drink, and I will give your camels drink also.' By this will I know which woman is to be Isaac's wife."

At the very moment Eliezer finished praying, a beautiful young woman came to the well. Eliezer watched as she went down to the well, filled her pitcher, and returned. As she passed him, Eliezer said, "Please let me have a little water from your pitcher."

The girl took the pitcher from her shoulder. "Drink, sir," she said. When he had finished drinking, she added, "I will draw water for your camels also."

The girl emptied her pitcher into the trough and returned to the well for more water. Eliezer watched until all ten camels had finished drinking. Then he gave the girl a gold ring and two bracelets and asked, "Whose daughter are you?"

"I am Rebekah, the daughter of Bethuel," she said.

Eliezer knew that Rebekah was Abraham's niece, and he knew she should become Isaac's wife. He bowed down his head and prayed: "Blessed be the Lord God of Abraham. He has led me to the house of my master's relatives."

Hearing this, Rebekah ran to tell her family about the stranger at the well. Laban, her brother, ran back to the well and took Eliezer to their home.

When it was time for dinner, Eliezer refused to eat. He said, "I will not eat until I have told you why I have come."

Laban said, "Speak on."

"I am Abraham's servant," Eliezer said, "and

I have come to find a wife for his son Isaac." Then Eliezer told them of his journey and his prayer to find the woman the Lord had chosen for Isaac. He explained how Rebekah had said exactly what he had asked.

"And now," Eliezer said, "tell me if this is to be."

Laban and Bethuel said, "Take Rebekah to be Isaac's wife, for it is the Lord's will."

Eliezer once more bowed himself to the ground and thanked the Lord for answering his prayer. Then he gave the rest of the presents he had brought to Rebekah and her family. Filled with rejoicing, the family ate and drank and celebrated.

The next morning Eliezer said, "Send me away so that I may return to my master."

"No!" Rebekah's mother said. "Let the girl stay at least ten days."

Eliezer replied, "Let us go, for this is of the Lord."

Rebekah's mother was very sad. How could she let Rebekah leave so soon? She knew she would never see her daughter again.

"Let her stay a little longer," she said.

But Eliezer still felt he should leave. So the family asked Rebekah, "Will you go with this man now?"

Rebekah answered, "I will go."

Before she left, they gave Rebekah a blessing like the one the Lord had given Abraham: "Be the mother of thousands of millions, and let your descendants possess the gate of those who hate them."

After the blessing, Rebekah traveled with Eliezer to the promised land. As they neared the land of Abraham, Rebekah saw a man walking in the fields.

"Who is that coming to meet us?" she asked.

Eliezer answered, "It is my master, Isaac."

Hearing this, Rebekah covered her face with a veil. Then she got down from the camel and met the man the Lord had chosen to be her husband.

—

GENESIS 24

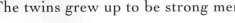

JACOB AND ESAU

Isaac and Rebekah had been married twenty years, but they had no children. They wanted children very much. They prayed and waited and hoped. Finally the Lord answered their prayers.

Before the child was born, Rebekah felt something was different. She prayed and asked what was happening.

"You will have twins," the Lord said. "Two nations will come from them. One nation will be stronger. The oldest son will serve the youngest."

When the time came, the twins were born. The first baby was red and hairy. They called him Esau, which means "hairy." The second brother was born holding onto Esau's heel. He was called Jacob, which means "following."

The twins grew up to be strong men. But they were very different from each other. Esau was a hunter. He did not keep the commandments. He married two wives who worshipped idols. Jacob was a farmer. He was faithful to the Lord.

One day Esau came home from hunting. He was very hungry and tired. He asked Jacob for a dish of pottage.

"I will give you the pottage if you will sell me your birthright," Jacob answered.

"I am near death," Esau said. "What good will this birthright do me?" So he sold his birthright.

Isaac was growing old. He could not see. He knew it was time to give his priesthood blessing. This blessing was usually given to the oldest son. But Esau had rebelled against the ways of the Lord. He had sold his birthright. What should

Isaac do? Isaac decided to give Esau the blessing anyway.

Isaac called Esau to him. "Take your bow and your quiver. Hunt me some venison," Isaac said. "Cook the meat the way I like it. Then bring it to me to eat. Then I will bless you before I die."

When Rebekah heard what Isaac said to Esau, she was troubled. She knew Esau was not worthy. The Lord had told her that Jacob was to be the ruler.

Calling Jacob to her, Rebekah told him what she had heard. "Go now to the flock and fetch me two goats," she said. "I will prepare meat for your father. You shall take it to him to eat. Then he will bless you."

"But Esau is a hairy man," Jacob said. "I am not. My father will feel me and know that it is not Esau."

Rebekah said, "Only obey my voice and bring me the meat."

Jacob brought the meat. Rebekah cooked it the way Isaac liked. She also baked bread.

When the food was ready, she dressed Jacob in Esau's clothing. She put goat skins on Jacob's arms, hands, and neck. Then she gave Jacob the food and sent him to his father.

"My father," Jacob said.

"Who are you, my son?"

"I am Esau. I have done as you asked me. Eat of my venison that your soul may bless me."

"Come here, please, that I may feel whether you are my son Esau or not."

Jacob stepped closer.

"The voice is Jacob's voice," said Isaac, "but the hands are the hands of Esau."

So Isaac ate the meal Jacob had brought. Then he gave Jacob the birthright blessing.

Soon after this, Esau arrived with his meat. "Let my father eat of his son's venison that your soul may bless me," Esau said.

"Who are you?" Isaac asked.

"I am your son Esau."

Isaac trembled and said, "Who? Where is he that brought me venison?
I blessed him."

After finding out what had happened, Isaac said, "Yes, Jacob shall be blessed."

When Esau heard these words, he cried with bitter tears. "Bless me, my father. Jacob took away my birthright. Now he has taken away my blessing."

"Behold, I have made him your master. What shall I do to you, my son?" Isaac asked.

"Bless me also," Esau said. Then lifting up his voice, he wept again. Seeing his son's sadness, Isaac gave Esau a father's blessing.

After that Esau hated his brother. He decided that when his father died, he would kill Jacob. When Rebekah learned this, she was afraid. She called Jacob to her and told him what Esau was planning. "Now, my son, obey my voice. Flee to Laban my brother. Stay with him until Esau's anger is turned away."

Isaac agreed and called Jacob to him. "You shall not take a wife of the daughters of Canaan," Isaac said. "Go to Haran and take a wife from the daughters of Laban."

Jacob prepared for the journey. Then before he left, Isaac gave him another blessing. "God bless you and give you the blessing of Abraham," Isaac prayed.

Thus Jacob fled to save his life and to find a righteous wife.

—

GENESIS 25–28

J A C O B ' S   W E D D I N G

After traveling many days, Jacob came to a well at the edge of a town. Three flocks of sheep were waiting to be watered.

"What place is this?" Jacob asked the shepherds.

They answered, "This is Haran."

"Do you know Laban, the grandson of Nahor?" Jacob asked.

"Yes, we know him."

"Is he well?" Jacob asked.

"Yes, he is well," they said. "Rachel, his daughter, is coming now with her sheep."

When Jacob saw his cousin Rachel coming, he moved the rock from the well and began to draw water for her sheep. When Rachel came near, he greeted her with a kiss. "I am Jacob, the son of Rebekah, your father's sister," he said.

Rachel ran home to tell her father that Rebekah's son had come. Laban ran to the well to greet Jacob. He took Jacob in his arms and told him how happy he was to see him. Then he took him to his home.

For the next month Jacob lived with Laban's family. He helped with the work, and he got to know his cousin Rachel and her older sister, Leah.

At the end of the month, Laban asked, "Tell me, what pay shall I give you?"

Jacob answered, "I will work for seven years if you will give me Rachel to be my wife."

Laban said, "It is good."

Jacob worked for Laban for seven years, but he loved Rachel so much the years seemed like only a few days. At the end of the seven years, Jacob said to Laban, "Give me my wife, for I have kept my promise."

So Laban gathered his family and friends together and held a great feast to celebrate the marriage of his daughter. In the evening, Laban brought the bride to Jacob. She was wearing a veil over her face, so Jacob did not know the bride was Leah, not Rachel.

The next morning, Jacob saw that his new

wife was Leah. He was very angry. "What have you done to me?" Jacob asked Laban. "I worked for seven years for Rachel. Why have you tricked me?"

Laban answered, "In this country, the older daughter must marry before the younger, so I gave you Leah. Leah's wedding party will last a week. At the end of the week, I will also give you Rachel if you agree to work for me seven more years."

Jacob agreed, and the next week Rachel also became his wife.

As the years went by, Leah had four sons, whom she named Reuben, Simeon, Levi, and Judah. But Rachel had no children. This made her very sad.

She begged Jacob, "Give me children, or I will die."

Jacob answered, "I am not God. I am not keeping you from having children."

Rachel said, "Marry my maid, Bilhah. She will have children for me."

So Bilhah became Jacob's third wife. She had two sons, Dan and Naphtali.

When Leah saw this, she became very jealous. She had not had any more children, so she gave her maid Zilpah to Jacob. Zilpah had two sons, Gad and Asher. But then

Leah also had two more sons, Issachar and Zebulun, and a daughter, Dinah.

After many years, Rachel finally had a son. She named him Joseph.

Soon after Joseph was born, Jacob finished his years of working for Laban. He said to Laban, "Now I will go to my own country."

"Please stay," Laban said. "I have learned that the Lord blesses me because of you."

"But how will I provide for my family?" Jacob asked.

"What shall I give you?" Laban asked.

Jacob answered, "Give me nothing. I will serve you seven more years for cattle, sheep, and goats."

So Jacob worked seven more years for Laban. Finally, after twenty-one years, Jacob took his wives, children, flocks, and herds and returned home to Canaan. When Jacob arrived in Canaan, he asked Esau to forgive him. Esau had repented. He hugged Jacob, and the two brothers were at peace.

Some time later, God changed Jacob's name to Israel. Israel means "one who prevails with God." All the descendants of Jacob, or Israel, are called the children of Israel.

—

GENESIS 29–33

After awhile Israel's family moved to Bethlehem. While they were there, Rachel gave birth to a son named Benjamin. Israel rejoiced to have a twelfth son. But the joy was soon swallowed up in sorrow, for after the birth of her son, Rachel died.

Israel missed Rachel very much and treasured the two sons she had given him. The older brothers saw how much their father loved Joseph and Benjamin. They were very jealous. Israel gave Joseph a beautiful coat of many colors, and the brothers' jealousy turned to hatred.

To make matters worse, Joseph had dreams that he would be a ruler over his brothers. In one dream, all twelve brothers were binding sheaves in the field. Suddenly the eleven sheaves belonging to the brothers bowed down to Joseph's sheaf. In another dream, the sun and the moon and eleven stars all bowed to Joseph.

When Joseph told his brothers of his dreams, they hated him even more. "Are you to rule over us?" they cried.

One day, Joseph's brothers were away tending the flocks. Israel called Joseph to him and said, "Please take food to your brothers and see how they are doing."

Joseph left to find his brothers. When his brothers saw him coming, they said, "Here comes the dreamer! Let's kill him and throw him into a pit. Then we will tell Father that an evil beast has eaten him up."

But Reuben, the oldest brother, said, "Do not shed his blood, but throw him into this well."

When Joseph came near, the brothers attacked him. They ripped the beautiful coat from his back and threw him into the well. Some of the brothers still wanted to kill Joseph. As they argued about what to do, a caravan of Ishmeelite merchants approached. The caravan was carrying slaves, spices, and other goods to Egypt.

Judah asked his brothers, "What good will it do us to kill our brother? If we sell him to these Ishmeelites, we will get money for him."

The brothers agreed. They sold Joseph for twenty pieces of silver. When he was gone, they took Joseph's coat and splattered it with goat blood. Then they hurried home to show the coat to Israel.

"Oh, Father," they lied, "Joseph has been killed by a wild beast."

From that day on, Israel mourned for his son Joseph.

—

GENESIS 37

Joseph was taken by the Ishmeelites to Egypt. There they sold him to Potiphar, a captain of Pharaoh's guard.

Joseph had faith that God would help him. He worked hard at Potiphar's house and was honest. Potiphar came to trust Joseph so much that he put him in charge of his whole house.

Then Potiphar's wife fell in love with Joseph. She said, "Lie down with me."

Joseph said, "No! I will not sin against my master and against God!"

Every day Potiphar's wife asked again. Each day Joseph said no. One day before Joseph went to the house to do business, Potiphar's wife sent all the servants away. When Joseph came, she grabbed him by his cloak and begged him to lie with her. Joseph ran away, but she held tightly to his cloak and tore it from him. Calling to the servants, she said, "The Hebrew mocks us! He came to lie with me, but I cried out for you!"

When Potiphar came home, his wife showed him Joseph's cloak and told her story.

Filled with anger, Potiphar threw Joseph into prison.

But Joseph did not become bitter. He trusted God, worked hard in prison, and obeyed the guards. The keeper of the prison came to trust him so much that he put Joseph in charge of the whole prison.

Pharaoh's chief butler and Pharaoh's chief baker were prisoners, too. One night the butler and the baker both had dreams. They knew the dreams must mean something important, but they didn't know what their dreams meant. Because of this, they were unhappy. When Joseph came to them the next morning, he asked, "Why do you look so unhappy?"

"We have dreamed," they said, "and there is no one to tell us what our dreams mean."

"Do not meanings belong to God?" Joseph asked. "Tell me your dreams."

"In my dream," the butler said, "I saw a vine, and the vine had three branches. There were blossoms and ripe grapes, and Pharaoh's cup was in my hand. I took the grapes and made wine for Pharaoh's cup and gave it to Pharaoh."

Joseph said, "This is the meaning. The three

branches stand for three days. After three days, Pharaoh will free you from prison and give you back your job. You will give him his cup of wine as you did before. When you are freed, tell Pharaoh about me."

Then the chief baker said, "I also dreamed. I had three white baskets on my head. The top basket held all kinds of baked goods for Pharaoh. But birds came and ate them."

Joseph said to the baker, "The three baskets stand for three days. In three days, Pharaoh will hang you on a tree, and the birds will eat your flesh."

On the third day, Pharaoh freed the chief butler from the prison and hanged the chief baker. But the butler forgot to tell Pharaoh about Joseph.

Two more years went by, and then one night Pharaoh dreamed about cows and sheaves of grain. When he awoke, he was greatly troubled. He wondered what the dream meant. He called for all the wise men of Egypt, told them his dream, and asked what it meant. But the wise men could tell him nothing.

Then the chief butler remembered how Joseph had known the meaning of his dream. At last he told Pharaoh, and Pharaoh sent for Joseph. Joseph shaved, put on clean clothes, and hurried to Pharaoh.

Pharaoh said to him, "I have dreamed two dreams, but no one can tell me what they mean. The butler says you can tell the meaning."

Joseph explained, "It is not me that knows, but God shall give Pharaoh an answer."

"In the first dream," Pharaoh said, "I stood on the bank of the river. Seven healthy, fat cows came out of the river and ate grass. Seven other cows also came out of the river, but they were skinny and starving. The seven starving cows ate the seven fat cows. But after they had eaten, they were still thin and starving. Then I awoke. When I fell asleep again, I had another dream. This time seven full, good ears of grain came up on one stalk. Then seven thin, withered ears of grain came up and ate the good ears."

Joseph said, "The dreams are the same. God has shown Pharaoh what he is about to do. The seven good cows and good ears of grain are seven years of plenty. The seven starving cows and withered ears of grain are seven years of famine. God is telling Pharaoh that there will come seven years of plenty. Then will come seven years of famine. Pharaoh should save grain during the seven good years so that there will be food during the seven bad years. Pharaoh should put a wise man in charge of saving the grain."

Pharaoh said, "Because God has shown you all this, there is none as wise as you. You shall be in charge of my house. You shall rule over all the people. Only I will be greater than you."

Then Pharaoh took off his ring and put it on Joseph's hand. He put fine linen clothes on Joseph and a gold chain about his neck. He ordered Joseph to ride in the second chariot, the one directly behind Pharaoh's chariot. He made him ruler over all the land of Egypt. To show that Joseph had a new master, Pharaoh gave him an Egyptian name, Zaphnath-paaneah. He also gave him Asenath to be his wife.

Joseph was seventeen years old when his brothers sold him into slavery. For thirteen years he had been either a slave or a prisoner in Egypt. Now he was thirty years old, and he was suddenly a ruler of Egypt. Still Joseph remained faithful to God and prayed to him for help in all he did. Joseph traveled through the land, gathering food. He made storehouses in the cities and fields and collected so much grain that he could not count it all.

During the seven good years, his wife, Asenath, had two sons. Joseph named the first son Manasseh, meaning "God has made me forget." Joseph named him this because he said that God had made him forget all his trials. Joseph named the second son Ephraim, meaning "fruitful." Joseph chose this name because God had caused him to be fruitful in Egypt.

When the seven years of plenty ended, the famine began. But with Joseph's help, Pharaoh and the Egyptians were prepared. Joseph opened the storehouses and sold grain to the people so that they did not go hungry.

—

GENESIS 39–41

In the land of Canaan the famine grew very bad. Fearing his family would starve, Israel called his sons to him. "I have heard that there is grain in Egypt," he said. "Therefore, go to Egypt and buy grain so that we will not die."

And so Joseph's ten elder brothers journeyed to Egypt.

When the brothers arrived, they were sent to Joseph, who sold all the grain. As they entered his presence, they bowed down before him. As they did, Joseph recognized them. He remembered his dream in which their sheaves had bowed down before his. But his brothers did not recognize him.

Joseph asked them in Egyptian, "Where are you from?" Then a servant spoke the words in Hebrew for his brothers.

The brothers answered, "From the land of Canaan. We have come to buy food."

Joseph cried, "You are spies!"

This frightened his brothers. They said, "No, my lord! We have come to buy food. We are honest men and are all sons of the same man. There are twelve brothers in our family. The youngest stayed home with our father, and another is dead. We are the ten eldest."

"I do not believe you!" Joseph said. And he had the brothers cast into prison.

After three days, the brothers were brought again to Joseph. He said to them, "So that I will know if you are honest men, let one of your brothers be bound in the prison. The others may carry grain back to your home. If you want the brother who remains to return to you, you must bring your youngest brother to me. Then I will know you are not spies."

When the brothers heard this, they began to speak among themselves in Hebrew, not knowing that Joseph could understand. They said, "This trouble has come upon us because of what we did to Joseph."

Reuben said, "I told you not to sin against the boy! Now his blood is required of us."

When Joseph heard this, he turned himself away and wept. After awhile he turned back, bound Simeon, and sent him to prison. Then Joseph commanded his servants to fill his brothers' sacks with grain. He also had them put each man's money back into his sack. Then the sacks were loaded upon donkeys, and the brothers departed.

Along the way, one of the brothers opened his sack to feed some grain to his donkey. When he saw the money, he cried out to his brothers, "My money is here!"

The brothers were baffled and frightened.

Did the Egyptians know of this? Did the Egyptians think they had stolen the money? Would they follow them? Would they throw them into prison again?

The brothers returned to Canaan in a great hurry and told their father all that had happened. When Israel heard that Zaphnath-paaneah wanted the brothers to take Benjamin back to Egypt, he was sorely grieved. He cried, "Joseph is gone! Simeon is gone! Now, if you take Benjamin away—oh, these things are against me!"

Reuben said, "I will take Benjamin to Egypt. If I do not bring him back to you safely, you may kill my two sons."

Israel answered, "Benjamin shall not go down with you. His brother is dead, and he is the only son of Rachel's that is left to me. If harm comes to him, then I will die of sorrow."

But after a time, the family ate all the grain that was brought from Egypt. Calling his sons to

him once again, Israel asked them to go back for more grain.

The brothers said to him, "Zaphnath-paaneah said to us, 'You shall not see my face, except your brother be with you.' If you will send Benjamin with us, we will go down to buy food. If you will not send him, we will not go."

Israel was greatly troubled by this. Without food, they would all die. But he could not bear the thought of losing Benjamin. Then Judah said: "Send the boy with me. I will bring Benjamin safely back to you."

Israel answered, "If it must be so, do it. Take honey, myrrh, and almonds as a present for the man, and take double the money to pay him. Perhaps your money was given back to you by mistake."

So the brothers once more made the trip to Egypt. When Joseph saw them return with Benjamin, he ordered his servants to bring them to dine with him.

The brothers did not know what Joseph wanted. They were frightened as the servants

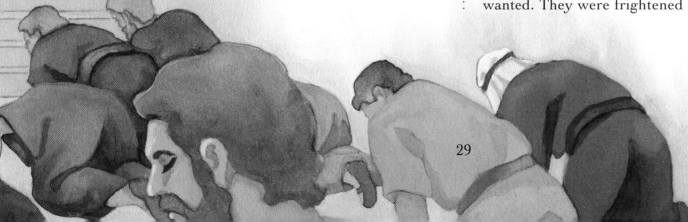

29

took them to Joseph's house. They worried that there would be trouble because of the money that had been found in their sacks. When they came near the door, they began to apologize to the steward of Joseph's house. They tried to give the money back. They explained, "We did not steal the money. It was found in our sacks. We do not know how it got there."

The steward said, "Peace be to you. Fear not. Your God has given you treasure in your sacks."

Then the steward brought Simeon to them. Joyfully the eleven brothers greeted one another. As they explained to Simeon all that had happened, the steward took the men into Joseph's house. He gave them water to wash their feet. Still fearful, they prepared the presents they had brought and waited.

At noon, Joseph appeared. He had his servant ask them in Hebrew, "Is your father well? Is he still alive?"

They bowed down to Joseph and answered, "Our father is in good health."

Turning to Benjamin, Joseph said, "God be gracious unto you, my son." Then, hastily, he went back to his chambers and wept. When he

was through weeping, he washed his face and went back to eat.

The Egyptians did not like to eat with the Hebrews, so there were three tables set. Joseph ate by himself at one table. The Egyptians sat at another table, and the eleven brothers sat at a third table. The brothers marveled, for they were seated at the table in order of birth, starting with the firstborn, Reuben, and going down to Benjamin. Joseph sent them food from his table, but to Benjamin he gave five times as much. Slowly the brothers began to relax and to drink and be merry with Joseph.

After the meal, Joseph again commanded the steward to fill his brothers' sacks with as much food as they could carry. He again had their money put in their sacks. But he also ordered his steward to put a silver cup that belonged to Joseph into Benjamin's sack.

At the first light the following morning, the brothers left. As soon as they had gone, Joseph said to his steward, "Get up and follow the men. When you have overtaken them, say to them, 'Why have you rewarded good with evil?'"

The steward did as he was told. Soon he found the brothers. "Someone has stolen my master's silver cup!" he said, and he demanded to search their sacks.

The brothers said, "Your master has been good to us. Why would we steal from him? If one of us has taken the cup, he will die. The rest of us will become your master's slaves."

Knowing they were innocent, they took down their sacks and opened them. How surprised they were when on top of the grain they found their money and, in Benjamin's sack, the silver cup. The brothers were stricken with grief. They tore their clothes to show how grieved they were, and they returned to Joseph's house and fell upon the ground before him.

Joseph's servant demanded, "What deed is this that ye have done?"

Judah replied, "What shall we say? How shall we clear ourselves? We will be your servants."

Joseph said, "God forbid that I should do so. But the man in whose hand the cup is found, he shall be my servant. The rest of you go in peace to your father."

Then Judah stepped close to Joseph and cried, "Oh, my lord! Let me, your servant, speak to you. And do not let your anger burn against me."

Joseph said, "Speak on!"

Judah spoke: "My lord, you asked us to bring our brother. We told you this would grieve our father. But you said, 'Except your youngest brother come with you, you shall see my face no more.' And so we told our father your words. Our father answered that his wife Rachel had given him two sons. The one had been torn in pieces and taken from him, and now, if harm came to the other, he would die of sorrow."

Judah continued, "Therefore, if I return without the boy, our father will surely die. I promised I would bring him back. Therefore, please let me be your servant instead."

At these words, Joseph could no longer

31

keep his secret. He knew his brothers were sorry for the terrible thing they had done to him. Tears filled his eyes. He sent away all his servants. When the servants were gone, Joseph said in Hebrew, "I am Joseph. Is my father still alive?"

His brothers were so astonished they could not answer.

Joseph said, "Please come close to me."

When they had drawn near, Joseph said again, "I am Joseph, your brother, whom you sold into Egypt. But do not grieve because you sold me. God sent me to Egypt to save your lives and the lives of your children. God has made me a father to Pharaoh and a ruler over all the land."

The brothers could hardly believe what they were hearing.

Joseph continued, "Now, hurry back to my father and tell him that his son Joseph is ruler of all Egypt. Then come back and live with me. Bring your families and flocks, and I will take care of you, for there are yet five years of famine."

As the brothers began to understand his words, Joseph hugged Benjamin and wept. Then, rejoicing but still weeping, he hugged and kissed each of them, and they wept with him.

Later, Joseph gave them wagons and food, and they returned to Canaan to tell their families the wonderful news.

When the brothers returned, they said to Israel, "Joseph is yet alive. He is governor over all the land of Egypt."

At first Israel did not believe them. But they showed him the gifts Joseph had sent and told him Joseph's story. "It is enough," Israel finally said. "Joseph my son is alive! I will go and see him before I die."

And so it happened that Israel and his children packed their belongings and traveled to Egypt to be reunited with their brother. When they drew near to the city, Joseph made ready his chariot and went out to meet his father. The two men hugged and wept and rejoiced greatly to be together again.

When Pharaoh discovered that Joseph's family had come to Egypt, he gave them the land of Goshen. Israel lived in Egypt for seventeen more years. Then he died at the age of 147.

Before Israel died, however, he gave a father's blessing to each of his children. He also blessed Manasseh and gave Ephraim, Joseph's youngest son, the birthright.

—

GENESIS 42–49

For more than four hundred years the children of Israel lived in Egypt. After that long, the Egyptians didn't remember who Joseph was. Even worse, the new Pharaoh was afraid of the Israelites because there were so many of them. He feared they would take over the whole country. So Pharaoh made them slaves. He put them to work making bricks out of mud and straw.

The children of Israel worked long and hard every day. Their life became bitter. But still, the Israelites had many babies. This worried Pharaoh even more. He ordered the midwives, who were named Puah and Shiphrah, to kill all the baby boys that were born to the Israelites. But Puah and Shiphrah refused to obey. When Pharaoh saw they were not killing the babies, he asked them why. They told him the Israelite women were very strong and had their babies before the midwives could get there.

Because Puah and Shiphrah loved God more than Pharaoh, God blessed them greatly. But Pharaoh now commanded that every son born to the Israelites should be cast into the river.

After Pharaoh made this law, an Israelite woman named Jochebed had a son. She loved the child and would not let him be thrown into the river. Instead she risked her own life by hiding him.

As the baby grew, it became harder and harder to hide him. Finally, when he was three months old, Jochebed made a basket of

33

bulrushes, coated it with pitch to make it waterproof, and put the baby inside. Then she placed the basket among the reeds in the River Nile. The baby's older sister, Miriam, watched to see what would happen to him.

The daughter of Pharaoh and her handmaidens came to the river to bathe. There the daughter of Pharaoh found the basket.

She ordered one of her maids, "Bring the basket to me." Wading into the bulrushes, the maid pulled the basket to the place where the daughter of Pharaoh waited. They lifted the lid to see what was inside. As the basket opened, the tiny baby cried out. The sound filled the princess's heart with compassion. She said, "This is one of the Israelite children. I will keep him as my son." She named the child Moses, which means "drawn from the water."

Miriam stepped out from her hiding place. "Shall I go and find one of the Israelite women to nurse the child for you?" she asked.

"Yes, go," Pharaoh's daughter answered.

Miriam ran home and told Jochebed all that had happened, and they returned to the princess.

Pharaoh's daughter said to Jochebed, "Take this child and nurse him for me, and I will pay you." Jochebed agreed to care for the child that would be known as the son of Pharaoh's daughter.

Living in the palace, Moses was raised as an Egyptian prince, but in his heart he knew he was one of the children of Israel. One day he was out walking among the Israelite slaves, watching them work. He saw an Egyptian beating a slave. He was angry to see the man being treated this way. He was so angry he killed the Egyptian and buried his body in the sand.

The next day Moses saw two Israelite men fighting. He asked the man who had done the wrong, "Why are you fighting with your brother?"

The slave answered, "Who made you a judge over us? Will you kill me as you did the Egyptian?"

Moses was afraid. People knew what he had done. Soon the news reached Pharaoh. Pharaoh became angry and decided to kill Moses. When Moses heard this, he fled Egypt to escape from Pharaoh.

—

EXODUS 1–2

After he left Egypt, Moses journeyed for many days. Finally he came to a well in the land of Midian. There he stopped to rest and drink. Seven daughters of the priest of Midian arrived to water their father's sheep. As the women began to fill the water troughs, other shepherds arrived. They drove away the women's sheep and herded their own flocks to the troughs.

Seeing this, Moses defended the women. He drove away the shepherds and then helped the women gather their sheep.

When the daughters returned to their father, Jethro, he asked, "Why are you back so soon today?"

They answered, "An Egyptian delivered us out of the hand of the shepherds and drew water for us."

"Where is he?" Jethro asked. "Why did you leave him there? Go tell him to come and eat with us!"

And so it was that Moses came to stay with Jethro's family. After awhile Moses married Jethro's daughter Zipporah. They had two sons. Jethro gave Moses the Melchizedek Priesthood. Moses tended sheep and lived happily with his wife and family.

Then one day Moses led his flock of sheep to a mountain called Sinai. There he saw a bush burning with fire. But the bush was not burned up by the fire. Moses turned aside to look more closely at the bush. As he went near the bush, the Lord called to him from the midst of it: "Moses, Moses!"

Moses answered, "Here I am."

The voice said, "Draw no closer. Take off your shoes, for the place where you stand is holy ground."

Moses removed his shoes.

The voice continued, "I am the God of your father, the God of Abraham, the God of Isaac, and the God of Jacob."

Moses hid his face in fear, but the Lord went on speaking: "I have seen the affliction of my people in Egypt and have heard their cries. I know their sorrows. I am come down to deliver them out of the hand of the Egyptians and to bring them into a good land. You are to go to Pharaoh and bring my people out of Egypt."

Moses asked, "Who am I that I should go to Pharaoh? How can I bring forth the children of Israel?"

The Lord said, "I will be with you. Pharaoh will not let you go. But I will stretch out my hand and smite the Egyptians with wonders. Then he will let you go."

Moses said, "But they will not believe that God has appeared to me."

"What is in your hand?" the Lord asked.

Moses answered, "A rod."

"Cast it on the ground," the Lord commanded.

Moses obeyed, and as the rod fell to the ground it became a serpent. The sight of it frightened Moses.

The Lord said, "Put forth your hand, and take the serpent by the tail."

When Moses did so, it became a rod again.

Then the Lord said, "Now put your hand inside your robe against your chest."

Moses obeyed, and when he took his hand out, it was white with leprosy.

"Put your hand inside your robe again," the Lord said.

This time, when Moses removed his hand, it was whole again.

"If they will not believe these two signs," the Lord said, "you shall take of the water of the river. Pour it on the dry land, and the water shall become blood."

Moses said, "But I am slow of speech!"

God answered, "Who made man's mouth? Have not I, the Lord? I will teach you what to say."

Moses pleaded, "O my Lord, please send someone else."

"Is not Aaron your brother?" the Lord asked. "I know that he speaks well. You shall teach him, and he shall speak for you. I will teach you all that you shall do."

When Moses finished speaking with the Lord, he returned to Jethro. He said to Jethro, "Let me go, for I must return to my brethren in Egypt."

"Go in peace," Jethro said. So Moses returned to the land of Egypt with the rod of the Lord in his hand.

—

EXODUS 2–4

Many times the Lord came to Moses to teach him. One day the Spirit took Moses to a high mountain. There the glory of God fell on Moses. This gave him power to stand in God's presence. Thus Moses saw and talked with the Lord face to face.

The Lord said, "I am the Lord God Almighty. You are my son. I have a work for you to do, Moses, my son."

Then the Lord showed Moses the world. He saw all the people of the world. He marveled at this vision. But when the Lord withdrew, Moses lost his strength. Falling to the earth, Moses lay helpless for many hours.

Moses said, "My spiritual eyes have seen God. His glory was upon me."

As Moses spoke, Satan came to him. "Moses, son of man, worship me," Satan said.

"Who are you?" Moses asked. "I am a son of God. I am like his Only Begotten Son. Where is your glory that I should worship you?"

Then Moses continued, "Blessed be the name of my God. His Spirit has not withdrawn from me. I can judge between you and God. Get behind me, Satan. Deceive me not."

Suddenly Satan began to rant and rave. "I am the Only Begotten, worship me," he shouted.

As Satan raged, fear crept into Moses' heart. But remembering God, he prayed and received strength. "Leave me, Satan," Moses said, "for I will worship only God."

At these words, Satan began to tremble. The earth shook. "In the name of Jesus Christ," Moses commanded, "leave me, Satan."

Hearing this command, Satan cried with a loud voice. Then, weeping, wailing, and gnashing his teeth, he left.

When Satan was gone, Moses prayed.

"Blessed are you, Moses," the Lord answered. "For I, the Almighty, have chosen you. I am with you. I will be with you to the end of your life. You shall deliver my people from bondage."

Then Moses saw and heard many marvelous things. He wrote these things in a book. But because of the wickedness of men, the book was lost. When Heavenly Father restored the gospel, the book was also restored.

—

MOSES 1

In Egypt, Moses and Aaron met with the elders of Israel. They showed the elders the signs the Lord had given them. By these things, the people knew the Lord had heard their prayers. They knew he was about to set them free.

Next Moses and Aaron went to Pharaoh. At that time, Moses was eighty years old. Aaron was eighty-three.

Moses and Aaron said to Pharaoh, "The Lord God of Israel says, 'Let my people go, so they can make sacrifices to me in the wilderness.'"

Pharaoh answered, "I do not know the Lord, and I will not obey him. Why do you take the people from their work? Go to your work!"

That day Pharaoh gave new orders to the taskmasters of the people: "Do not give the people straw to make brick. Let them gather straw for themselves. Make them work harder."

Now the people had to find straw themselves. But they still had to make as many bricks. When the people were unable to make enough bricks, the taskmasters beat them.

The Israelites cried out to Pharaoh, "Why are you doing this?"

Pharaoh answered, "Because you have so much idle time, you want to sacrifice to your God."

Then the people said to Moses, "You have just given Pharaoh more reason to hate us!"

Moses did not know what to do, so he prayed to the Lord: "Lord, why did you send me? Since I spoke to Pharaoh, he has done evil to this people. He has not set them free."

The Lord answered, "It is time. Now you shall see what I will do to Pharaoh. I hear the groaning of my children. I remember my covenant. Say to the children of Israel, 'The Lord will set you free. He will lead you to the promised land.'"

But when Moses told the people what the Lord said, they would not listen. They were too afraid. The Lord told Moses, "Go again and ask Pharaoh to let the children of Israel go."

Moses and Aaron did as the Lord commanded. As they came close to Pharaoh, Aaron threw his rod down on the floor. It became a serpent. When Pharaoh saw this, he called his wise men and magicians. They threw their rods down, and they also became serpents. But Aaron's serpent swallowed the others. Even this did not soften Pharaoh's heart. He told Moses

and Aaron to leave, and he would not let the people go.

Again the Lord commanded Moses to go to Pharaoh. So Moses and Aaron went back. This time, Aaron struck the river with his rod. The waters of the entire land turned to blood. Even the water in the jars in people's houses became blood.

After seven days, all the fish in the river died. The stink filled the air. Again Moses and Aaron went to Pharaoh. They said, "The Lord says, 'Let my people go that they may serve me.'" But Pharaoh hardened his heart and refused.

Aaron then held out his rod, and millions of frogs came out of the ponds and rivers. They hopped into the houses, into the people's beds,

and even into their bread dough. Everywhere there were frogs and frogs and more frogs! The people cried out for Pharaoh to do something. Pharaoh called for Moses and Aaron. He said, "Beg the Lord to take the frogs away from us. Then I will let your people go."

So the frogs died. Only those in the river were left. But when Pharaoh saw that the frogs were gone, he again hardened his heart and would not let the children of Israel go.

Again the Lord spoke to Moses and Aaron: "Stretch out your rod, and smite the dust so that it becomes lice in all of Egypt."

Aaron did as he was commanded, and lice crawled over every man and beast in Egypt. When the magicians of Pharaoh saw this, they said to Pharaoh, "This is the work of God." But

Pharaoh's heart was hardened, and he would not listen to them.

Then the Lord said to Moses, "Rise up early in the morning and stand before Pharaoh. Say to him, 'The Lord says, if you do not let my people go, I will send swarms of flies upon you and your people and your houses. But there will be no flies upon my people in the land of Goshen. Then you will know that I am the Lord.'"

Soon swarms of flies tormented all the people of Egypt. However, just as the Lord promised, there were no flies in the land of Goshen. When Pharaoh saw this, he called for Moses and Aaron again. He said, "Sacrifice to your God in this land."

Moses answered, "That is not good. We will go three days' journey into the wilderness. There we will sacrifice to the Lord our God as he commanded us."

Finally Pharaoh said, "I will let you go."

Moses answered, "I will ask the Lord to take away the flies. But do not lie to me again."

As soon as the flies left the land, Pharaoh hardened his heart once more. He told the people they could not go.

Again Moses went to Pharaoh. He said, "The Lord God of the Israelites says, 'Let my people go, that they may serve me. If you will not, then sickness will come upon all your cattle and horses and donkeys and camels and oxen and sheep.'"

The next day, many of the Egyptians' animals were dead. But not one animal belonging to the children of Israel died. Still Pharaoh hardened his heart and would not let the people go.

Then the Lord said to Moses and Aaron, "Take handfuls of ash from the furnace. Let Moses throw the ash toward heaven where Pharaoh can see it. It will become a dust that will cause boils to break out on every man and beast in the land of Egypt."

Moses threw the ashes into the air, and all the people and animals of Egypt were cursed with painful boils. Still Pharaoh hardened his heart and would not let the Israelites go.

The Lord said to Moses, "Hold out your hand toward heaven, that there may be hail in all the land of Egypt."

Moses held out his hand, and thunder cracked. Hailstones fell upon the land of Egypt. The storm ruined crops and trees and killed many animals. But in the land of Goshen there was no hail.

Pharaoh called for Moses and Aaron and said, "I have sinned. The Lord is righteous, and

I and my people are wicked. Ask the Lord to take away the thunder and hail. Then I will let you go."

Moses said, "As soon as I am out of the city, I will spread my hands to the Lord, and the thunder and the hail will stop. But I know you will not obey the Lord God."

Moses then went out of the city and spread his hands to the Lord. The thunder and hail stopped. But when Pharaoh saw that the storm had ended, he would not let the people go.

Again Moses and Aaron went to Pharaoh. They said, "The Lord God of the Israelites says, 'How long will you refuse to be humble before me? Let my people go that they may serve me. If you do not, tomorrow I will send locusts. They shall cover the face of the earth so that no one can see the ground. They will eat every tree and everything the hail did not destroy.'"

Pharaoh's servants pleaded, "Let the men go. Do you not know that Egypt is destroyed?"

So Pharaoh asked Moses, "Who will go?"

Moses said, "We shall go with our young and old, with our daughters, our flocks, and our herds."

Pharaoh answered, "No! Only the men shall go." And Pharaoh sent Moses and Aaron away.

Now Moses stretched out his hand, and the locusts came, eating every plant the hail had not destroyed. As the locusts darkened the face of the earth, Pharaoh called for Moses and Aaron. He said, "I have sinned against the Lord your God and against you. Please forgive me. Ask the Lord to take away these locusts."

Moses asked the Lord to take away the locusts. A strong wind came up and blew the locusts into the Red Sea. But as soon as the locusts were gone, Pharaoh again hardened

41

his heart. He would not let the children of Israel go.

Now the Lord commanded Moses to stretch out his hand toward heaven. As he did so, a thick darkness fell upon the earth. For three days the Egyptians had no light. Only the children of Israel had light in their homes.

Again Pharaoh called for Moses. He said, "Go, serve the Lord. Take your children, but leave your flocks and your herds."

Moses answered, "We need our flocks and our herds for sacrifices. Our cattle also shall go with us."

Pharaoh became very angry. He said, "Get away from me! If you come here again, you shall die!"

Moses answered, "I will not come here again." And he left.

Then the Lord said to Moses, "I will bring one more plague upon Egypt. Then Pharaoh will let you go. Speak now to the people."

So Moses told the people all that the Lord commanded. He told every family to cook a male lamb for a feast. This lamb was a symbol of Jesus Christ, who would be sacrificed for the sins of the world. They roasted the lamb over a fire. Then they ate all of it so that none was left for the next day. They also ate unleavened bread. For seven days they did not even keep leaven in their houses.

They ate the feast standing up with their shoes on. They dressed in their traveling clothes. They held a staff in their hands as if ready to work. And they ate the meal in haste.

God also told them to paint the side posts of their doors and the lintels over the doors with the lamb's blood. He said, "Do not go out the door until morning." The children of Israel obeyed.

That night all the firstborn children in the land of Egypt died. Even the firstborn son of Pharaoh died. But in the houses with blood on the doors, no one died.

In the middle of the night, Pharaoh called for Moses and Aaron. "Get away from my people!" he cried. "Go serve the Lord as you have said!"

Moses told the people what Pharaoh had said. In a great hurry, they gathered their belongings and fled from the land of Egypt.

"Remember this day," Moses said to the people. "For the Lord has set you free. This day shall be called Passover. It will help you remember that death passed over your houses."

—

EXODUS 4–12

After the children of Israel had gone, Pharaoh was angry. He cried, "Why have I done this? Why have I let Israel go from serving us?"

Taking his soldiers and six hundred chariots, he hurried after the Israelites.

The Israelites were camped by the Red Sea. They saw the approaching army. They were frightened by the many soldiers. They forgot all the marvelous signs and miracles they had seen. They forgot the promises of the Lord.

They cried to Moses, "What have you done to us? It would have been better to serve the Egyptians than to die here in the wilderness!"

"Fear not," Moses said. "Stand still and see the salvation of the Lord, which he will show you this day."

Then Moses lifted his rod and stretched his hand out over the sea. As he did this, the waters of the Red Sea parted to make a pathway. "Go!" Moses commanded.

The children of Israel stepped onto dry ground. They herded their flocks and carried their belongings between the high walls of water.

Pharaoh and his army followed, driving their chariots between the parted waters. Moses watched until the last Israelite had safely crossed over. Then he stretched forth his hand again, and the water fell over Pharaoh and his army. The water covered all the Egyptian soldiers, chariots, and horses that were in the Red Sea. At last the children of Israel were free.

—

EXODUS 14

43

After they crossed the Red Sea, the Israelites were very grateful. They sang praises to God and danced with joy. Miriam, the sister of Moses, took a timbrel and led the women in dancing and rejoicing. "Sing ye to the Lord," she cried, "for he has triumphed gloriously."

Then the people began their journey in the wilderness. They traveled for three days without finding any water. Finally, they came to a spring in the land of Marah, but the water was so bitter they could not drink it.

The people asked, "What shall we drink?" And they began to murmur against Moses for taking them out of Egypt.

Again Moses prayed to the Lord. In answer, the Lord showed him a tree and told him to throw it into the water. When Moses threw the tree into the water, the water became sweet. The people drank the water and again moved on.

But less than two months later, the people again murmured against Moses and Aaron.

They cried, "We wish we had died in Egypt! At least there we had bread to eat."

Again the Lord spoke to Moses: "I will rain bread from heaven. The people shall go out and gather enough for each day. But on the sixth day they shall gather twice as much so they shall have enough for the Sabbath. In the evening there shall be quails so that they will have meat."

The next morning, when the children of Israel went out, there was something white, like drops of dew, all over the ground. When the people saw it, they called it manna, which in Hebrew means "What is this?"

Moses said, "This is the bread the Lord has given you to eat. Gather only enough for one day, and eat it all."

So the children of Israel gathered manna and ate until they were filled. But some of the Israelites were not obedient. They were greedy. They gathered more than they needed for one day. The next morning the manna they saved was crawling with worms, and the stink of it filled their tents.

On the sixth day, the people gathered twice as much manna as they needed. On the next day, the Sabbath, it was still good. But again some of the people did not obey. On the sixth day they gathered enough for only one day. The next morning when they went to gather manna, there was none, so they went hungry.

One day the armies of Amalek came against the children of Israel. Joshua led the battle

while Moses, Aaron, and Hur watched from the top of a hill. As long as Moses held up his hands, the Israelites won the battle. But when Moses lowered his hands, Amalek began to win.

For a long time Moses stood with his hands held high. But his arms grew weary, and he could no longer hold them upright. Seeing that the Israelites would lose the battle, Aaron took one arm and Hur the other. Together they held Moses' hands high. When the sun went down, the Israelites won the battle.

Thus the miracles of the Lord continued. By day the Lord led the children of Israel with a cloud and by night with a pillar of fire. He protected and guided them as they made their way through the wilderness.

—

EXODUS 15–17

After three months the Israelites came to a mountain called Sinai. This was the same mountain where Moses saw the burning bush and first spoke with the Lord. The people pitched their tents at the foot of the mountain. They camped there for about a year. During this time Moses climbed the mountain often to speak with the Lord.

The first time Moses went up the mountain, the Lord gave him a message for the people. He said, "Tell the people that if they will obey my covenant, they shall be a special treasure to me. They shall be a kingdom of priests."

Moses came down from the mountain. He gathered the elders of Israel and told them what the Lord said. The elders answered, "We will do all the Lord has said."

Moses went up the mountain again to speak with the Lord. The Lord said, "Go to the people. Sanctify them today and tomorrow. Have them be ready the third day, and I will come down where they can see."

Moses came back down the mountain and told the people what the Lord said. "Repent and purify yourselves," he said. "Be ready on the third day."

On the morning of the third day, thunder and lightning tore through the sky. A thick cloud hovered over the mountain. The sound of a great trumpet blared through the air. The noise was so loud the people trembled with fear. But despite their fear, they followed Moses to the bottom of the mountain to meet God.

As they drew near the mountain, they saw a strange thing. The mountain was covered with smoke. The smoke went up into the sky like the smoke of a fiery furnace. As they drew closer, the mountain shook, and the sound of the trumpet grew louder. The glory of the Lord shone like fire on the top of the mountain. The people became even more frightened.

Moses left the people at the bottom of the mountain. He climbed to the top to talk with God. The noise and fire went on, but now the people could hear God speaking.

"You shall have no other gods before me," God said.

"You shall not make yourselves any graven image.

"You shall not take the name of the Lord your God in vain.

"Remember the Sabbath day, to keep it holy.

"Honor your father and your mother.

"You shall not kill.

"You shall not commit adultery.

"You shall not steal.

"You shall not bear false witness.

"You shall not covet."

The people were so frightened to hear the voice of God and to see the lightning and the fire and hear thunder and the trumpet that they moved away from the mountain. They said to Moses, "You speak to us, and we will listen. But do not let God talk to us, because we might die."

Moses answered, "Do not be afraid, for God is come to prove you." But the people moved even farther from the mountain.

After that, Moses climbed the mountain often to talk with the Lord. Sometimes he went alone, and sometimes the Lord commanded him to take others with him. He always brought back instructions from the Lord for the people.

One time, Moses went up into the cloud that covered the mountain and stayed for forty days and forty nights. While he was there, the Lord wrote the Ten Commandments and the Celestial Law on two stone tablets.

But while Moses was on the mountain, the children of Israel forgot about God. They gave Aaron all their gold jewelry and any other gold they had. Aaron melted it and made a golden calf. After the idol was finished, the people worshipped the calf. They held a great feast and sacrificed to the golden idol. Filled with worldly desires, the people ate and drank and began to dance and sing around the golden calf.

On the mountain, Moses could hear the noise. He wondered what the people were doing. Finally the Lord said to him, "Go down, for the people have become wicked. I will destroy this people and make of you a great nation."

But Moses prayed, "Lord, turn away your anger. The people will repent of this evil. Please do not come against them."

The Lord answered, "If they will repent of the evil which they have done, I will spare them.

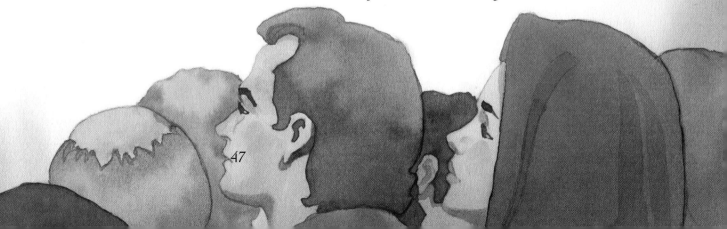

But you shall punish all those who will not repent of evil."

So Moses went down from the mount with the two stone tablets. But as he drew near the camp, he saw the calf and the people worshipping it. He became so angry he threw the tablets to the ground and smashed them. Then he took the calf and burned it. When it was melted, he ground the gold to powder and cast the powder into the water. Then he made the children of Israel drink the water.

Moses asked Aaron, "Why have you led this people to do evil?"

Aaron answered, "They asked for gods, because they didn't know what had become of you. They gave me their gold. I cast it into the fire, and out came this calf."

Moses was very sad to see such wickedness. He commanded the people to repent. The next day, he said to them, "You have sinned a great sin. Now I will go up to the Lord, and perhaps I can make an atonement for your sin."

When Moses returned to the Lord, he said, "These people have sinned a great sin, and have made gods of gold. But please forgive their sin. If not, blot me out of your book."

The Lord answered, "Whosoever sins against me, I will blot him out of my book."

Moses returned and told the people that if they would repent, the Lord would be with them again.

The Lord commanded Moses to make two more tablets of stone and to take them to the top of the mountain. Moses stayed on the mountain fasting and praying for forty days. While he was there, the Lord wrote the words of the law again upon the stone tablets. But this time he did not write all of the law. The people had proved themselves unworthy when they worshiped the golden calf. Because of their sin, they could not have the Celestial Law or all of the priesthood blessings.

After the forty days, Moses went down with the new tablets. The elders of Israel waited anxiously for Moses at the bottom of the mountain. But as he drew near them, the men saw that Moses' face shone with the glory of God. This frightened Aaron and the others so much they refused to go near him. In order to calm them, Moses veiled his face. Thus covered, he taught the people the things the Lord had commanded him to teach.

—

EXODUS 19–34;
DEUTERONOMY 4–5;
JST EXODUS 34

The Lord helped the Israelites many times while they traveled in the wilderness. He showed them many miracles. After so many miracles, they should have trusted him. But after each miracle the people forgot the Lord and murmured against Moses.

Once, when the people murmured and complained, the Lord sent fiery serpents among them. When a serpent bit someone, that person became very sick, and many died.

The people cried out to Moses, "We have sinned, for we have spoken against the Lord and against you! Pray to the Lord that he will take away the serpents!"

So Moses prayed. In answer, the Lord said, "Make a serpent of brass, and set it upon a pole. When someone is bitten, have him look at the brass serpent, and he will live."

Moses made the brass serpent. He put it on a pole and put the pole in the middle of the camp. Then he told the people to look at the serpent and they would be healed. But the children of Israel would not do it. That was too easy! They would not believe that just looking at a brass serpent could heal their terrible fevers and pain.

Finally, the Lord said he would not let these people enter the promised land. He would wait for them all to die. Then he would let their children and grandchildren enter the promised land. So the children of Israel wandered in the wilderness for forty years. After forty years, the people who would not obey the Lord all died. Their children and grandchildren were ready to move on.

But the Lord did not let Moses go with them. Moses' work on earth was over. Instead of entering the promised land, he was translated and taken into heaven.

The new leader of the people was Joshua. The Lord said to Joshua: "As I was with Moses, so I will be with you. I will not fail you nor forsake you. Be strong and courageous and do all that Moses commanded you. Turn not from the law, and you will prosper wherever you go."

So Joshua prepared the people to enter the promised land.

—

NUMBERS 14, 21, 27;
DEUTERONOMY 34;
1 NEPHI 17:40–42

While they waited to enter the promised land, the children of Israel camped on the east side of the River Jordan. They carried with them the Ark of the Covenant. Across the river was the city of Jericho. The people of Jericho were worried about the thousands of people camped on the other side of the river. They had heard of the miracles of God. They had heard of the many battles the Israelites had won.

Joshua called two men to him. He said to them: "Go and look at the land and the city of Jericho. Then come back and tell me what you see."

The two spies stole across the river. They went through the gate into the city, pretending to be travelers. While they were there, they watched the people and they listened to what they said. Before the spies left, it grew dark. The gate of the city was closed, so they could not leave. They found a place to stay at the house of a woman named Rahab. There they waited for the morning to come.

But word reached the king of Jericho that two Israelites had come into the city to spy. The king sent soldiers to Rahab's house. The soldiers demanded, "Bring forth the men! They are spies!"

But Rahab had seen the soldiers coming and had hidden the men under stalks of flax on her roof.

Rahab told the soldiers, "Two men came to me, but I didn't know where they were from. They left at dark and went out the gate before it was closed. If you hurry, you can still catch them."

When the king's men left, Rahab hurried to the roof and told the spies what had happened.

She said, "I know the Lord has given you this land. The people of Jericho are fainting with fear of you. We know the Lord dried up the water of the Red Sea for you, and your God is God in heaven and in earth."

Rahab continued, "Since I was kind to you and hid you, please be kind to me and my family. Save my family from death."

The spies answered, "We will protect you if you tell no one about us."

Rahab agreed. Then she told the men, "Get to the mountain before the soldiers find you. Hide there three days. After the soldiers return to Jericho, go your way."

The spies thanked Rahab. They said, "When we come into the land, hang this scarlet thread in your window. If you do this, all that are in your house will be saved."

Rahab said, "I will do as you say."

Rahab's house was on top of the city wall. She opened a window and let down a strong cord, and the spies climbed down and escaped.

Just as Rahab had said, three days later the soldiers gave up their search and returned to Jericho. As soon as they left, the spies hurried to Joshua. They told Joshua all that had happened and how the people of Jericho had

fainted with fear. They said, "Truly the Lord has given us all the land."

Early the next morning, Joshua told all the people to move close to the banks of the River Jordan. There they camped for three days while their leaders told them what to do. "When the priests move the Ark of the Covenant, follow it. But do not get close to it," the leaders said.

Then Joshua said to the people, "Sanctify yourselves, for tomorrow the Lord will do wonders among you."

The next day the people gathered at the river again. Carrying the Ark of the Covenant, the priests stepped into the waters of the Jordan. As their feet touched the water, the river parted and the water upstream gathered in a giant heap. The priests walked to the middle of the Jordan and stopped. There they waited while the children of Israel crossed the dry riverbed.

When everyone had crossed the riverbed, Joshua said to the priests who carried the Ark of the Covenant, "Come up out of the Jordan." The priests obeyed, and as they stepped out of the riverbed, the waters of Jordan came back together and flowed on their way.

As the people had crossed, one man from each tribe had taken a stone from the riverbed. On the other side, Joshua told the men to pile up the stones. Then he told the people, "When your children ask, 'What are these stones?' you shall tell them how the waters of the Jordan parted before the Ark of the Covenant." The crossing of the River Jordan took place at the time of Passover. So the Israelites then camped and held the Feast of the Passover. The next morning, when they awoke, there was no manna. They did not need it, because there was plenty of food in the promised land.

The Lord then commanded Joshua to take the city of Jericho. He told Joshua just how this was to be done. On the first day, all the men marched around Jericho. Seven priests, each bearing a trumpet made of a ram's horn, led the men. Behind the priests, other men carried the Ark of the Covenant. Behind them were the

men of war. They went around Jericho once and returned to the camp. On the second, third, fourth, fifth, and sixth days, they did the same thing.

On the seventh day they arose early in the morning and marched around the city seven times. After the seventh time, the priests blew their trumpets. "Shout, for the Lord has given you the city!" Joshua cried.

At the command, all the people shouted. Suddenly the mighty wall around Jericho fell down. With the wall gone, the Israelite army charged into the city and slew all the Canaanites. But there was one house with a scarlet thread in the window. Because of the thread, no soldier entered that house, and all the people inside were saved.

—

JOSHUA 2–6

52

After they conquered the land of Canaan, the Israelites were ruled by men and women who were called judges. One of the judges was named Gideon.

In the time of Gideon, the Israelites forgot the Lord. Because they had forgotten him, the Lord did not defend them against their enemies. The Midianites raided Israelite villages and towns. To protect themselves, the Israelites made caves in the mountains. During the day they tried to plant and grow crops and tend their animals. But at night, or when they saw the enemy coming, they hid in the caves.

After seven years of this, the Amalekites joined the Midianites and came against Israel. Together they swept through the country at harvest time. They destroyed everything they saw. When they left a town, there were no more crops, cattle, sheep, or other animals.

Hungry and frightened, the Israelites finally remembered the Lord. They prayed, "Save us, or else we perish."

The Lord answered their prayers by calling Gideon to lead them. One day, as Gideon was threshing wheat, the angel of the Lord came to him. The angel said, "The Lord is with you, mighty man of valor."

Gideon asked, "If the Lord is with us, why are we having this trouble? Where are his miracles of which our fathers spoke?"

Then the Lord said, "Go in your might, and you shall save Israel from the Midianites."

"How shall I save Israel?" Gideon asked. "My family is poor, and I am the least in my family."

"Surely I will be with you," the Lord said. "You shall smite the Midianites as if they were one man."

Gideon said, "If this is God's will, then show me a sign that I might know. Do not leave until I return with a present and set it before you."

"I will wait," he said.

Quickly Gideon prepared goat meat, cakes, and broth. He brought them to the angel.

The angel said, "Take the flesh and the cakes. Lay them on this rock. Then pour the broth over them."

Gideon did as he was told. Then the angel touched the meat and cakes with his staff. Fire came out of the rock and burned up the food. Then the angel disappeared.

That same night the Lord said to Gideon, "Break down the altar to Baal that your father has made. Then cut down the grove of trees that is by it. In place of the altar, build an altar to the Lord. Then offer one of your father's bullocks as a burnt offering. Use the wood of the grove to make the fire."

Gideon rose up and, taking ten servants, did as the Lord commanded him.

The next day, the men of the city saw that the altar of Baal was destroyed. They were angry. "Who did this?" they asked.

"Gideon!" one of the crowd answered.

The men hurried to Gideon's father, Joash, and said, "Bring out your son, so we can kill him."

"If Baal really is a god," Joash said, "then let him punish the person who broke down his altar." And so the men left Gideon alone.

A while later, the Midianites and the Amalekites came against the city. Gideon sent

messengers through all the land to gather men for the army. However, Gideon needed to be sure that this was God's will. He wanted to know that God would help him win the battle. "I will put a fleece of wool on the floor," he prayed. "If I am to save Israel, then let the dew in the morning be on the fleece, but let the earth beside it be dry."

Early the next morning, Gideon arose and hurried to the spot where he had left the fleece. Picking up the fleece, he wrung it until he had a bowl full of water. When he looked at the earth around the fleece, he saw that it was dry.

Then Gideon said to God, "Please do not be angry with me, but let me know once more. Tomorrow let the fleece be dry, but on the ground around it let there be dew."

The next morning Gideon again hurried to

54

the spot. The fleece was dry, and the ground was covered with dew. Now Gideon knew that God would be with him.

Soon thirty-two thousand men came to fight against the Midianites. But the Lord said to Gideon, "You have too many men. If I let them defeat the Midianites, they will think they did it by their own strength. Therefore, tell the men that if they are afraid to fight, they may go home."

Gideon did as he was told. Twenty-two thousand men left to return home. But again the Lord said, "The people are yet too many. Take them to the water and let them drink."

Gideon took his men to the water to drink. There Gideon watched as some of the men knelt and lapped the water like dogs. Others gathered water in their hands, lifted the water to their mouths, and drank from their hands.

"By the three hundred men that drank from their hands will I save you," God said. "Let all the others go."

That same night the Lord said to Gideon, "Go down to the Midianites and hear what they say."

So Gideon took Phurah, his servant, and they sneaked into the camp of the Midianites by night. Gideon saw that the Midianite army was so large they were like hordes of grasshoppers. Even their camels were as numerous as the sand of the sea. This frightened Gideon, but as he sneaked closer he heard one of the Midianites tell of a dream he had.

The man said, "A cake of barley bread fell into the host of Midian and smote a tent so that it overturned."

Another man answered, "This is nothing else save the sword of Gideon. For God has delivered Midian into his hand."

When Gideon heard this, he worshipped God and returned to the camp of Israel. "Arise," he said, "for the Lord has delivered into your hand the host of Midian."

Gideon gave each man a trumpet and an empty pitcher with a lighted lamp inside it. "Do as I do," he said.

Gideon and his three hundred men stole through the darkness to surround the Midianite camp. At Gideon's command, his men blew their trumpets and broke their pitchers so that the light shone in the darkness. They shouted, "The sword of the Lord and of Gideon!"

The Midianites and Amalekites thought that each light and trumpet was an army. Frightened, they grabbed their swords and began to fight.

But in the dark they could not tell which army a man belonged to, and they began to fight each other. Gideon and his men followed the soldiers that ran away and killed them. Thus, with only three hundred men, the Lord saved the children of Israel once again.

—

JUDGES 6–7

SAMSON

Another of the judges of Israel was Samson. Samson could have been a great leader if he had been true to the Lord. But he was not.

The Israelites turned from the Lord, and for forty years they were in bondage to the Philistines. Finally the people again began to pray and to seek the Lord. In answer to their prayers, the Lord sent a young man named Samson into the world. Samson, it was prophesied, would deliver Israel from the Philistines.

When Samson was born, his parents were told that he was to be a Nazarite. This meant that his life would be dedicated to the Lord. The men and women who were Nazarites made special vows with the Lord. To show that they were not part of the world, they never cut their hair or drank liquor of any kind. They also promised to do no unclean thing. As part of his covenant with Samson, the Lord gave Samson a gift of strength. However, he warned Samson that if he broke his Nazarite covenants, he would lose his strength.

Samson was stronger than any other man. Once Samson was on top of a hill called Etam. An army of Philistines came to find Samson. There were three thousand Israelite soldiers, but they were afraid of the Philistines. So they went to the top of Etam to get Samson. They said, "We have come to tie you up and give you to the Philistines."

So they tied Samson with cord and took him to the Philistines. But the Spirit of the Lord came upon Samson. He easily broke the cords from his arms. Then he took the jawbone of a donkey and with it killed a thousand Philistines. When the battle was over, he threw away the jawbone. He was terribly thirsty, and he cried,

"You have helped your servant kill all these men, but now shall I die of thirst?"

So God made water spring from a hollow place in the rock, and Samson drank and was revived.

Samson judged Israel for twenty years. The Philistines grew to hate Samson more and more because of his strength and the many things he did against them. So they plotted to destroy him.

The Philistines knew that Samson loved a Philistine woman named Delilah. Some of them went to Delilah and said, "Find out why Samson is so strong. Find out how we can win against him. If you do this, each of us will give you eleven hundred pieces of silver."

Delilah agreed and began to question Samson. She said, "Please tell me what makes you so strong."

Samson answered, "If I am bound with seven new cords that were never dried, then I shall be weak."

So the Philistines brought Delilah seven new cords, and then they hid nearby. When Samson was asleep, she tied him up. Then she cried, "The Philistines are here, Samson!" Instantly Samson broke the cords off his arms as if they were merely threads.

Delilah said, "You have tricked me and told me lies. Please tell me how you can be bound."

"If they bind me with new ropes that were never used," Samson said, "then shall I be as weak as other men."

So Delilah took new ropes and bound Samson. Then she cried, "The Philistines are here!" As soon as he heard the words, Samson broke the ropes off his arms as if they were threads.

Delilah said, "You have tricked me and told me lies again. Tell me how you can be bound."

Samson said, "If you weave my hair with the web of the loom and fasten it with a pin, then I will be weak."

So while Samson slept,

Delilah wove his hair with the web and fastened it with a pin. When she was finished, she cried, "The Philistines are here!"

Samson arose and walked away with the pin and the web in his hair.

"How can you say you love me?" Delilah said. "You have tricked me three times, and you have not told me what makes you so strong."

She begged and begged until Samson finally gave in. "My hair has never been cut," he said. "If my head is shaved, then my strength will go from me and I shall be weak like any other man."

Again the Philistines came. This time, while Samson slept with his head on Delilah's lap, a man shaved off his hair. When the hair was gone, Delilah cried, "The Philistines are here!"

"I will go out as at other times," Samson said, not knowing that the Spirit of the Lord had left him. The Philistines captured him. They blinded his eyes and took him to Gaza. There they bound him with brass chains and threw him into prison. But as the months passed, Samson repented. The hair of his head grew back and he became strong again.

One day the Philistines gathered to offer sacrifice to their god Dagon. During the celebration they cried, "Our god has saved us from our enemy who slew many of us." Then they called for Samson so they could make fun of him.

When Samson was brought from the prison, he asked the boy who held him, "Let me feel the pillars that hold up the building so I can lean on them."

There were about three thousand people on the roof. They all began to make fun of Samson. While they laughed and jeered, Samson cried out to the Lord, "O Lord God, remember me, I pray, and make me strong this once that I may be avenged of the Philistines for my two eyes."

As he prayed, Samson took hold of the two middle pillars that held up the building. "Let me die with the Philistines," he said. Then he pushed with all his might on the pillars, and the house fell, killing Samson and the Philistines.

—

JUDGES 13–16

RUTH AND NAOMI

During the time of the Judges, there was a famine in the land of the Israelites. Elimelech and his wife, Naomi, lived in Bethlehem with their two sons, Mahlon and Chilion. To find food, they moved to another country called Moab.

The ways of the people in Moab were very different. They worshipped strange gods. At times they had warred against Israel. Even so, the Moabites welcomed the family.

After some time, Elimelech died. This left Naomi in a strange land with their two sons. Mahlon grew up and married a woman named Ruth. Chilion married Orpah. Ruth and Orpah were Moabites, but they gave up their false gods and worshipped the God of Israel. Naomi loved Ruth and Orpah, and they loved her.

Then Naomi's sons also died. Without her husband and sons, Naomi grew homesick. She longed to be back in her own country and among her own people. So when the famine in Israel ended, Naomi decided to go back to Bethlehem. Ruth and Orpah asked to go with her.

Naomi said to them, "Return to your mothers' houses. And may the Lord deal kindly with you as you have with me."

"We want to go with you to your people," Orpah and Ruth said.

"Why will you go with me?" asked Naomi. "I have no more sons to be your husbands."

Finally Orpah kissed Naomi good-bye and returned to her people. But Ruth said to Naomi, "Please don't ask me to leave you. Where you go, I will go, and where you live, I will live. Your people shall be my people, and your God my God."

Naomi could not refuse her. She took Ruth to Bethlehem. There she found a husband for Ruth from among her kinsmen. His name was Boaz. Ruth and Boaz were ancestors of Joseph, the stepfather of Jesus.

—

RUTH 1–4

Hannah and her husband, Elkanah, lived on the slopes of Mount Ephraim. Hannah had no children. This made her very sad. Often Hannah wept and didn't eat because her sorrow was so great.

Elkanah asked Hannah, "Why do you weep? And why do you not eat? Am I not better to you than ten sons?" Hannah knew this was true, but still she wanted children and could find no comfort.

Now, once each year, Hannah went with Elkanah to Shiloh to worship and to offer sacrifice to the Lord. One year, when they arrived in Shiloh, Hannah went to the temple to pray. "O Lord of hosts!" she silently prayed. "Look on the

affliction of your handmaid. Give me a man child, and I will give him to the Lord."

Hannah prayed for a long time. Her lips moved without sound. She wept, and her body rocked. After watching for awhile, Eli, the priest, decided she was drunk.

Eli asked her, "How long will you be drunk? Let the wine alone!"

Hannah answered, "I am a sad woman. I have not drunk wine or strong drink. But I have poured out my soul to the Lord."

Eli saw he had made a mistake. He said to Hannah, "Go in peace. And may the God of Israel give you what you ask."

Hannah returned home joyfully, and in

due time she had a baby boy. She named him Samuel, which means "heard of God." She loved him very much.

After Samuel was born, Elkanah got ready to go to Shiloh again. Hannah told him, "I will not go until Samuel is weaned. Then I will take him to live forever in the house of the Lord."

Elkanah said, "Do what seems good to you."

During the next years, Hannah cared for Samuel. Carefully she fed him and made clothes for him and taught him to love the Lord. But Hannah did not forget her promise. When Samuel was old enough, Hannah took him to Eli, the priest, at the temple.

She said to Eli, "I am the woman who stood here praying to the Lord. I prayed for this child, and the Lord sent him to me. For this reason, I now lend the boy to the Lord."

Hannah left Samuel with Eli, who would teach him. Samuel lived and worked in the temple. He learned the duties of the priest.

But Hannah did not forget Samuel. Each year she made him a new coat and went to Shiloh to visit him. Each year she marveled at how he had grown and the things he had learned. And just as Hannah did not forget Samuel, the Lord did not forget Hannah. He

blessed her with three more sons and two daughters. Now her joy was full.

As Samuel grew, he followed the commandments. Thus he became strong and wise. One night, while everyone was asleep, a voice called to Samuel and woke him.

"Here I am," Samuel answered, and ran to Eli. "You called me," Samuel said.

Eli answered, "I called not. Lie down again."

Samuel went back to his bed. He lay down and closed his eyes.

The voice called again, "Samuel!"

Again Samuel arose and went to Eli. "Here I am," he said.

"I called not, my son," Eli said. "Lie down again."

So Samuel returned to his bed. But a third time the voice called. Again Samuel went to Eli. "Here I am, for you did call me," Samuel said.

This time Eli knew that it must be the Lord calling. He said to Samuel, "Go, lie down. And when he calls you, say, 'Speak, Lord, for your servant hears.'"

So Samuel returned to his bed. This time the Lord came and stood beside him. "Samuel, Samuel!" the Lord said.

"Speak, for your servant hears," Samuel said.

Then the Lord told Samuel that Eli's sons

had been very wicked. Eli had not taught them right, and so his family would be cursed.

The next morning Samuel was afraid to tell Eli what the Lord had said. But Eli called Samuel to him and said, "What did the Lord say to you? Please, do not hide it from me." So Samuel told Eli.

When Samuel grew up, he became the judge of Israel. He did all that the Lord commanded, and the power of God was with him. Because of this, all Israel came to know that Samuel was not only the judge but also a prophet of God.

—

1 SAMUEL 1–3

KING SAUL

Samuel judged Israel for many years. He tried to teach the people about God. He tried to tell them it was wrong to worship idols. But most of the people would not listen. They grew more and more wicked. Even Samuel's sons would not obey the commandments. So when Samuel was old and it came time to appoint a new judge, the elders of Israel went to Samuel. They said to him, "You are old, and your sons do not walk in your ways. So give us a king, like the other nations have."

Samuel knew this was wrong, but the people insisted. So Samuel prayed to the Lord and asked what he should do.

"They have not rejected you," the Lord said.

"They have rejected me. Warn the people what will happen to them if they have a king. But give them what they want."

So Samuel told the people what a king would do. "A king will take your sons and daughters for his servants," he said. "He will take your fields, your vineyards, and your olive orchards. He will take your servants to be his servants. He will take your sheep. You will cry to the Lord to be free from him."

But the people would not listen to Samuel. They wanted to be like other nations. They wanted a king.

So the Lord said to Samuel, "Tomorrow about this time, I will send you a man from the land of Benjamin. Anoint him to be king over my people."

Now it happened that a young man named Saul was in the country. He was looking for his father's donkeys that had wandered away. Saul searched and was about to give up when his servant came to him. The servant said, "There is a man of God in the city. Let's go to him. Maybe he can show us where to find the donkeys."

When Samuel saw Saul coming, the Lord whispered to him, "This is the man of whom I spoke. He shall be king."

When Saul came to Samuel, Saul said, "Please tell me, where is the prophet?"

Samuel replied, "I am the prophet. Come and eat with me. I will tell you all that is in your heart. And do not worry about the donkeys. Someone has found them."

As they ate, Samuel said to Saul, "The Lord wants you to be king of Israel."

Saul was very surprised by this news. "I am of the smallest of the tribes of Israel," he said. "And my family is the least of all the families of the tribe of Benjamin. How can this be?"

But Samuel told Saul the Lord would help him. For the rest of the day, Samuel taught Saul and encouraged him.

The next morning before Saul left, Samuel anointed him king and blessed him. Then Samuel told Saul where to find his father's donkeys. Saul found the animals where Samuel had said. Then he returned home.

Saul was a good king at first. He was humble. He had the Spirit of the Lord with him, and he obeyed the prophet in all things. But after two years, Saul began to forget the Lord. Once before a great battle, Samuel said to Saul, "Go to Gilgal and wait seven days. After the seven days, I will come to you. I will pray for you and offer sacrifices before the battle."

Saul took his army and went to Gilgal to wait for Samuel. But huge armies of Philistines surrounded them. Many of Saul's men ran away in fear. Saul was afraid his whole army would leave him, and he did not want to wait longer. So Saul offered the sacrifice himself, even though he had no authority to do so.

As soon as he finished, Samuel came to him. Samuel asked, "What have you done?"

Saul answered, "I saw the soldiers leaving me, and you did not come. The Philistines were gathered against us. So I made the burnt offering."

Samuel said to Saul, "You have done foolishly. You did not keep the commandment of the Lord your God. The Lord would have made your kingdom last forever. But now your kingdom shall not continue."

Then Samuel left.

Later, Saul's army was about to fight the Amalekites. The Lord told Saul, "Destroy everything. Do not let any animals live, and do not take any spoils."

After the battle, Samuel came to Saul. "I have done what the Lord commanded," Saul said.

Samuel asked Saul, "Then why do I hear this bleating of sheep and the lowing of oxen?"

Saul said, "The people wanted to keep the best of the sheep and the oxen to sacrifice to the Lord. We destroyed all the rest."

Then Samuel said to Saul, "When you were little in your own sight, did not the Lord anoint you king over Israel? The Lord gave you commandments, but you did evil in his sight."

"No!" Saul said. "I have obeyed the Lord! I won the battle with the Amalekites. The people kept animals to sacrifice."

Samuel said to him, "Do you think the Lord wants sacrifices more than he wants obedience? To obey is better than to sacrifice. Because you reject the word of the Lord, he rejects you from being king."

After that, Samuel never came to see Saul again.

—

1 SAMUEL 8–15

Samuel was sad about what Saul had done. One day the Lord said to Samuel, "How long will you mourn for Saul? Fill your horn with oil, and go to Jesse in Bethlehem. You shall find a new king among his sons."

Samuel asked the Lord, "How can I go? If Saul hears of it, he will kill me."

The Lord answered, "Take a heifer with you. Say, 'I have come to sacrifice to the Lord.' Call Jesse to the sacrifice. Then I will show you what you shall do."

So Samuel took a heifer and went to Bethlehem. When he arrived, he told Jesse and his sons, "Come with me to the sacrifice."

Jesse and his sons went to the sacrifice. There Samuel met Jesse's oldest son, Eliab. Eliab was tall and handsome. Samuel thought, "Surely this is the man the Lord wants to be king."

But the Lord said to Samuel, "Pay no attention to how he looks or how big he is. I do not see as man sees. Men look at the outside of a man, but I look at the heart."

Then Jesse called another son, Abinadab. Samuel said, "The Lord has not chosen this man, either."

Jesse brought five more sons to Samuel. Samuel said, "The Lord has not chosen any of these. Are these all your children?"

"No," Jesse answered. "There is yet the youngest. He is tending the sheep."

Samuel said, "Bring him to me."

The youngest son was David. When Samuel saw David, the Lord said to Samuel, "Arise, anoint him. For this is he."

So Samuel took the horn of oil and anointed the boy David to be the king of Israel.

—

1 SAMUEL 16

DAVID AND GOLIATH

When David was still young, the Philistines were at war against the children of Israel. The Philistines had a mighty army. They had many chariots, and their spears and armor were better than any the children of Israel had. But even worse, the Philistines had a champion who was a giant. His name was Goliath. He was almost ten feet tall. On his head he wore a helmet of brass. He was covered with armor. He carried a huge spear.

Each day Goliath came close to the camp of Israel. He shouted, "Choose a man, and let him come out to fight me! If he kills me, we will be your servants! If I kill him, you will be our servants!"

These words filled the army of Israel with much fear. They

thought, Surely the Philistines and this giant will kill us! And they were afraid to fight.

Then one day, Jesse sent David to the Israelite camp to take food to his brothers. While David was there, Goliath came out to make fun of the Israelites. David asked his brothers, "Who is this Philistine, that he should defy the armies of the living God?"

When King Saul heard what David said, he asked to see David.

David said to Saul, "Don't be afraid of Goliath. I will go and fight him."

Saul answered, "You cannot fight him! You are but a boy, and he is a man of war."

"The Lord helped me kill a bear and a lion with my sling to save my sheep," David said. "He will save me from this Philistine."

Saul said, "Go, and the Lord be with you."

Then Saul said, "Use my armor and sword."

David tried on the king's armor and sword. "The armor is too heavy," he said. "And I do not know how to use the sword. I will use my sling."

So David found five smooth stones and put them in his bag. Then he went out to meet Goliath.

When Goliath saw a young boy coming, he cried, "I will feed you to the birds and to the beasts!"

But David was not afraid. He said to Goliath, "You come to me with a sword, with a spear, and with a shield. I come to you in the name of the Lord."

Goliath was filled with anger. He ran toward David with his spear lifted and ready to throw. David put a stone in his sling and flung it. The stone hit Goliath in the one place that was not covered with brass—the middle of his forehead. Goliath fell to the earth. David ran to the giant, took the sword from his hand, and cut off his head.

David had won the fight. But instead of surrendering and becoming the servants of the Israelites as Goliath had promised, the Philistines fled. But David's courage inspired the Israelites. Shouting loudly, they ran after the Philistines and won the battle.

—

1 SAMUEL 17

After slaying Goliath, David lived with Saul and served him. At first Saul loved David. He gave his daughter Michal to David to be his wife. Saul's son Jonathan became David's best friend. Saul made David the leader of his army. David won battle after battle for Saul. This should have pleased Saul. But when Saul saw how the people honored David, he became very jealous.

Saul was so jealous he made another man leader of the army. He hoped David would be killed in battle. But the Lord protected David. This only made Saul's jealousy grow. Twice he tried to kill David by throwing a javelin at him. Both times David moved away and was not hurt. David saw that he was no longer safe in Saul's house. So he left to find Samuel. For a time he stayed with Samuel. Then he went to hide in the wilderness.

Still Saul wanted to kill David. For years he hunted for David in the wilderness. Once after a long day of hunting, Saul fell asleep in a cave. He didn't know that it was the very cave in which David was hiding. When Saul was sound asleep, David stole from his hiding place. With his sword, David cut a piece of cloth from Saul's robe. But he would not hurt even a hair of Saul's head.

When Saul woke up and saw how David had spared his life, he wept and went away, sorry for how he had treated David. But his sorrow did not last long. After awhile he began to seek David's life once more. Again David found Saul sleeping, and again he would not hurt him. This time he took Saul's javelin and water bottle and ran to a nearby hill. David called to Saul from the hill. "The Lord gave you into my hand today," he said, "but I would not lift my hand against the Lord's anointed."

Saul answered, "The Lord bless you, my son David! You will do great things." And Saul stopped hunting for David.

About this time the Philistines saw how weak Israel was. Many of Saul's army had left to join David. The people no longer trusted or loved Saul. So the Philistines gathered a large army and marched against Israel. During the battle, the Philistines killed Saul and three of his sons. When the army of Israel saw that Saul was dead, they fled. Then the Philistines took over many of their cities.

At last David was king. He built a great

palace in Jerusalem. He drove the enemies of Israel out of the country. The people loved David. Israel became a great nation. The Lord also blessed David with many wives, children, and great wealth. Everything seemed to be perfect for David. But it did not last.

One evening David took a walk on the flat roof of his house. While walking, he saw a beautiful woman in a nearby yard and fell in love with her. He sent his servants to find out her name. They reported that she was Bathsheba, the wife of Uriah, one of David's soldiers. Knowing that Uriah was away in battle, David sent for Bathsheba.

Now David, who had been wise and strong and righteous, did something very selfish and sinful. He sent a message to Joab, who was in charge of the army. The message said, "Put Uriah in the front at the next battle, so he will be killed." Joab did as he was told, and Uriah was killed. Now David could marry Bathsheba.

But the Lord was angry with David for this great wickedness. The Lord sent Nathan the prophet to speak to David.

Nathan said to David, "There were two men in one city. One was rich, and the other was poor. The rich man had many flocks and herds. The poor man had nothing but one little lamb.

"One day a traveler came to visit the rich man. The rich man wanted to give his guest a good meal. But instead of killing a lamb from his own flock for the meal, he took the poor man's lamb and killed it."

When David heard this, he was very angry. "The man that did this thing shall surely die!" he said.

Then Nathan said, "You are that man! The Lord God of Israel says this to you: 'I made you king over Israel, but you would not obey my commandments. You killed Uriah and took his wife. Now the sword shall never depart from your house.'"

David cried out, "I have sinned against the Lord!"

For the rest of his life, David was sorry for the wrong he had done. But no matter how sorry he was or what else he did, he could not give back the life he had taken.

—

1 SAMUEL 18–2 SAMUEL 1

After David married Bathsheba, she had a baby boy. David called him Solomon, which means "peaceable."

As David grew old, the Lord chose Solomon to be the next king. David said to Solomon, "I am about to die. Be strong and follow the ways of the Lord. Keep his commandments, and he will bless you."

Solomon loved the Lord and obeyed his commandments. Because of this, the Lord came to Solomon one night in a dream and asked, "What shall I give you?"

Solomon answered, "O Lord my God, you made me king, but I am like a little child. I don't know enough to be king. Please give me an understanding heart to judge your people."

The Lord said to Solomon, "Because you did not ask for long life or riches or revenge upon your enemies, I will give you a wise and under-standing heart. And if you walk in my ways and keep my commandments, then I will also give you a long life."

One day after that, two women came to Solomon. One of them said, "This woman and I live in the same house. Each of us had a baby. But one night this woman rolled on her baby while in bed, and the baby died. Then she woke up in the night and saw what she had done. While I was sleeping, she took my son from beside me and laid him in her bed. Then she took her dead son and laid him in my bed. When I woke in the morning to feed my baby, he was dead. But it was not my son."

The other woman said, "Yes, it was! The living child is my son!"

The first woman said, "Not so! The living child is mine!"

The king listened to the women argue. Then he said to one of his servants, "Bring me a sword."

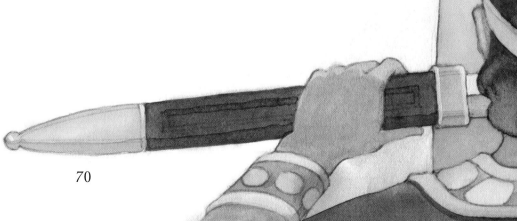

When the servant brought the sword, the king said, "Cut the baby in two. Give half to one mother and half to the other."

One of the women cried, "No! Give her the living child! Don't kill him."

But the other woman said, "Let it be neither mine nor hers, but divide it!"

Solomon then knew who the real mother was. He said, "Give the child to the woman who does not want it killed."

When the people of Israel heard about this, they knew that God had made Solomon wise.

—

2 SAMUEL 12–24; KINGS 3

THE PROPHET ELISHA

After King Solomon died, the kingdom of Israel was divided. The northern kingdom was still called Israel. The southern kingdom was called Judah. From that time on, each kingdom had its own king.

In Elisha's day, the king of Israel fought with Syria. Elisha helped Israel win. He told the king what the Syrians were going to do next. Thus the armies of Israel were ready and won.

The king of Syria was angry. He called for his servants. "Show me which of you is helping the king of Israel!" he said.

"None, my lord," one of the servants answered. "It is Elisha, the prophet. He tells the king of Israel the things you have planned."

So the king of Syria sent spies to find Elisha. They returned with the news that Elisha was in Dothan. During the night the king sent his soldiers to Dothan. The next morning Elisha and his servant awoke. When they went out, they were surrounded by soldiers.

The servant was filled with fear. "What shall we do?" he asked.

"Fear not," Elisha answered. "There are more on our side than on theirs."

The servant did not understand. He and Elisha were alone against an entire army. Then Elisha prayed, "Lord, please open his eyes that he may see."

Suddenly the servant saw that the mountain was covered with horses and chariots of fire.

71

As the soldiers came near, Elisha prayed again: "Please make these people blind."

Then the soldiers did not recognize Elisha. "Where is Elisha?" they asked.

"I will take you to him," Elisha said. Then he led them to the capital city of Samaria.

Once they were in Samaria, Elisha prayed, "Lord, please open the eyes of these men, so they may see."

The soldiers were surprised to find that they were in the middle of Samaria. The king of Israel was standing before them. These were their enemies!

"Shall I kill them?" the king asked.

"No," answered Elisha. "Feed them. Then let them go to their master."

So the king prepared a feast. After the men had eaten, he sent them away to their king.

—

2 KINGS 6

J O S I A H   T H E   B O Y   K I N G

Josiah was eight years old when he became king of Judah. His father and grandfather were wicked kings. But Josiah refused to follow their evil ways. Josiah wanted to serve the Lord. He wanted to obey the commandments. But he had not been taught the ways of the Lord. He did not know what to do.

When he was eighteen, Josiah wanted to restore the temple. He sent his scribe Shaphan to the priest Hilkiah with the orders. Hilkiah began the work. After some time he returned to Shaphan. "I have found the book of the law in the house of the Lord," Hilkiah said. He gave the book to Shaphan.

Shaphan took the book to King Josiah. Josiah asked Shaphan to read the scriptures to him. As Josiah heard the words, he was sad. He rent his clothes. This showed how sorry he was that his people were not keeping the laws. However, he was also happy that now he knew what to do.

"Ask the Lord about the words of this book," Josiah told Shaphan. "The Lord is angry because the people have not obeyed him."

Shaphan went to Huldah, the prophetess. He asked her about the words of the book. "This is the word of the Lord," Huldah said. "'Because Israel has forsaken me, I am angry. But to Josiah I say, Your heart is tender. You have humbled yourself before the Lord. Because of this, you shall not see the evil which will fall on this place.'"

Shaphan returned to King Josiah. He told him what the Lord had said. Josiah loved his people. He did not want evil to befall them. So when he heard the message, he told the people to meet at the temple. When they came, Josiah read the book of the law to them.

When he finished reading, Josiah made a covenant with the Lord. He promised that he would obey the commandments. Then he asked the people to covenant with the Lord. They did so.

Josiah then commanded that all the groves, the idols, and the false images be burned. There would be no more children sacrificed to idols. All the wicked priests were killed. Then he commanded the people to again celebrate the Passover and to remember God.

Never before or after was there a king like Josiah. He turned to the Lord with all his heart. But the people did not follow. So the anger of the Lord came upon them as Huldah had said.

A few years later, the king of Egypt waged war against Judah. During the battle, Josiah was killed. Thus he never saw the evil that came to his people.

—

2 KINGS 22–23

The people of Israel forgot God, so God did not defend them against their enemies. A people called the Assyrians conquered them and took them to Assyria. After awhile, the Assyrians let the people of Israel go, and the Israelites went into the north countries. The Bible does not tell what happened to them after that.

The Kingdom of Judah lasted longer. The Lord sent many prophets to teach the people of Judah. One of these prophets was named Lehi. The Book of Mormon tells the story of Lehi and his descendants.

Another of the prophets of Judah was Jeremiah.

When Jeremiah was very young, the Lord spoke to him and said, "Before you were born, I sanctified you and ordained you a prophet."

Jeremiah answered, "But I cannot speak. I am a child."

The Lord said, "Say not that you are a child. You shall go where I send you. Whatever I command you shall speak. Do not be afraid, for I am with you."

Then the Lord touched Jeremiah's mouth and said, "Behold, I have put my words in your mouth."

From that day forth, Jeremiah preached the word of God to the people. But the people were very wicked and would not listen. Jeremiah told the people Jerusalem would be destroyed if they did not repent. Still no one listened to him. They sacrificed their children to the false gods Baal and Moloch. They would not help the poor. They followed selfish desires and did all sorts of evil. No matter what Jeremiah did, they would not listen. This caused Jeremiah much sorrow.

Then, as Jeremiah had said, wars, drought, and famine came upon Judah. But even these did not cause the people to remember God. Instead of listening to Jeremiah's words, the people threatened to kill him. They locked him in stocks all night. They arrested him and tried him for blasphemy. They beat him and stoned him. False prophets stirred up the people against him, and King Zedekiah put him in prison. But Jeremiah knew the Lord was with him. He continued to preach the word of God.

Finally, just as Jeremiah had prophesied, Nebuchadnezzar, the king of Babylon, sent his armies. The armies destroyed Judah and took the people back to Babylon to be slaves.

—

JEREMIAH 1–52; 1 NEPHI 1

QUEEN ESTHER

About fifty years after the people of Judah were taken to Babylon, Persia conquered Babylon. The king of Persia was named Cyrus. Cyrus let the Jews go back to Jerusalem to rebuild their temple. But not all of the Jews returned. Some stayed in Babylon. Others went to Persia. That is how a Jewish girl named Esther and her cousin, a man named Mordecai, came to be in Persia.

By this time, Ahasuerus was king of Persia. It happened that Ahasuerus held a feast that lasted seven days. At the end of the seven days, Ahasuerus sent for his wife, Queen Vashti. He wanted her to come wearing her crown, to show her great beauty to the drunken men. But Vashti refused. Ahasuerus became angry. He said that Vashti was no longer queen. To find a new queen, he had the most beautiful women of the kingdom brought to him. From among them, he would choose a new queen.

Hundreds of beautiful women came to the palace in Shushan. For a year they bathed in special oils and dressed in beautiful clothing. In all ways they were made ready to be presented to the king. Then they went to King Ahasuerus to see if they would be the next queen of Persia.

Mordecai had brought up Esther as his own daughter. He knew that Esther was beautiful and also good. He wanted her to be queen. So Mordecai took her to the palace. The keeper of the women was very pleased with Esther. He gave her seven maids and the best room in the house of the women.

Finally the day came for Esther to be presented to the king, Ahasuerus. The king liked Esther very much and chose her to be the queen.

After Esther became queen, Mordecai learned that two of the king's servants were angry with the king. They were making plans to kill Ahasuerus. Mordecai told Esther and Esther told the king. Thus the king's life was saved.

Ahasuerus had a servant named Haman. Ahasuerus made Haman ruler over all the princes of Persia. When Haman came in or out of the gate, everyone bowed to him—everyone, that is, except Mordecai. This made Haman very angry. He looked for a reason to kill Mordecai. One day, Haman learned that Mordecai was a Jew. He thought if he could find a way to kill all the Jews in the kingdom, he would be rid of Mordecai.

He soon decided what he would do.

Haman said to King Ahasuerus, "There is a certain people in your kingdom that do not keep your laws. If it please the king, let them be destroyed."

The king agreed. He sent letters to all the provinces saying that in the twelfth month the Jews should be killed. When Mordecai heard this, he rent his clothes. He also put ashes upon his head and came to the king's gate. Esther's maids told her that Mordecai was outside wearing sackcloth. She sent clothes to him, but he would not wear them. So Esther sent her servant, Hatach, to find out what was the matter. Mordecai told Hatach what had happened. He gave Hatach a copy of the decree. He asked him to tell Esther to go to the king and plead for her people.

Hatach told Esther all that Mordecai had said. She sent Hatach back to Mordecai with another message: "You know that whoever goes to the king without being called is put to death unless the king holds out the golden scepter. The king has not called for me for thirty days."

Mordecai sent back a message. It read, "Who knows but that you are come to the kingdom for this very purpose."

When Esther read Mordecai's words, she knew what she must do. She sent another message to him: "Go, gather together all the Jews in Shushan and fast for me for three days. I and my maidens will fast also. Afterward I will go to the king. If I perish, I perish."

Mordecai did as Esther said.

On the third day of fasting, Esther put on her royal robes. She walked into the room where the king sat on his throne. Filled with fear, she waited to learn whether she would live or die. The room grew quiet and all eyes turned to her. What would the king do?

The king held out the golden scepter. Esther stepped forward and touched the top of it.

Ahasuerus asked, "What do you want, Queen Esther?"

Esther answered, "If it seems good, let the king and Haman come this day to the banquet that I have prepared."

The king commanded, "Tell Haman to hurry!" The king and Haman went to Esther's banquet.

As they were eating, the king again asked Esther, "What do you want? I will give you even half of my kingdom."

Esther replied, "If I have found favor in your sight, please let Haman and the king come to eat again tomorrow. Then I shall make my request."

Haman went home that night filled with pride. He gathered all his family and friends and boasted that the queen had asked him to join her for dinner. He told them he had been invited to dine again the next day.

But Haman complained, "Yet all this means nothing to me. As long as Mordecai the Jew sits at the king's gate and refuses to bow down to me, I cannot be happy."

Haman's wife, Zeresh, said, "Then let a gallows be made. Tomorrow ask the king to hang Mordecai." Haman thought this was a very good idea. He ordered the gallows to be built.

That night the king could not sleep. He

asked that the book of records be brought to him. He read the story of how Mordecai had helped save his life. He asked his servants, "What honor has been done to Mordecai for this deed?"

The servants answered, "Nothing has been done for him."

Then the king asked, "Who is in the court?"

Now, Haman had come and was waiting in the outer court to ask the king to hang Mordecai. The servant replied, "Haman stands in the court."

The king commanded, "Let him come in."

Haman entered, but before he could make his request, the king spoke: "What shall be done to the man the king wants to honor?"

Haman thought he was the man to be honored. He replied, "Give him the royal clothing the king used to wear. And bring the horse that the king rides upon. Place the royal crown upon the man's head. Have the most noble princes take him through the streets of the city. As he rides through the city, tell all the people what he has done."

This pleased the king. He said, "Make haste, Haman. Do all you have said to Mordecai the Jew."

Haman was furious at this turn of events.

But there was nothing he could do. He had Mordecai dressed in royal robes. Then he paraded Mordecai through the streets of the city. As they rode, Haman had to call out to all the people that the king wished to honor Mordecai. Then he had to tell them how Mordecai saved the king's life.

Glad to be done with the awful task, Haman went on to the banquet with Esther and the king. While they were eating, the king again asked Esther, "What do you want?"

Esther answered, "If I have found favor in thy sight, O king, let my life be given me. Let my people be spared, for we are to be destroyed."

Ahasuerus asked, "Who wants to do this to you?"

Esther answered, "Our enemy is this wicked Haman."

This news shocked Ahasuerus. Haman had told him the Jews were rebelling and were evil. Now he knew that Haman had lied. Ahasuerus ordered Haman to be hanged on the very gallows Haman had built for Mordecai. Thus Esther's courage saved not only herself but all of her people.

—

ESTHER 1–7

There was a man in the land of Uz whose name was Job. He was a perfect man who feared God and did no evil. Because of this, the Lord greatly blessed him. He owned 7,000 sheep, 3,000 camels, 500 yoke of oxen, and 500 donkeys. He had a lovely wife, seven sons, and three daughters.

One day the sons of God presented themselves before the Lord. Among them was Satan.

The Lord asked, "Where have you been, Satan?"

Satan answered, "I've been going to and fro in the earth and walking up and down in it."

The Lord asked, "Have you seen my servant Job? There is none like him in the earth. He is a perfect man."

Satan answered, "Yes, because you have made a fence about him and about his house. But put forth your hand now, and take away all he has, and he will curse you to your face."

The Lord said, "All he has is in your power. Only do not hurt Job himself."

So Satan went out from the presence of the Lord.

Soon a messenger came to Job's house with bad news. He said, "The oxen were plowing and the donkeys feeding beside them. Suddenly the Sabeans fell upon them and took them away. They also killed your servants with their swords. Only I have escaped to tell you."

While he was still speaking, another servant came. "Fire fell from the sky and burned your sheep and your servants," he said. "Only I have escaped to tell you."

While that messenger spoke, another came. "Three bands of Chaldeans fell upon the camels and took them away and killed the servants," he said. "Only I have escaped to tell you."

While he spoke, still another messenger came. He said, "Your sons and daughters were eating at their eldest brother's house. Suddenly a great wind knocked down the house. The house fell upon them, and they are dead. Only I have escaped to tell you."

When Job heard these words, he rent his

clothes, shaved his head, and fell upon the ground. "The Lord gave, and the Lord has taken away," he said. "Blessed be the name of the Lord."

Again there came a time when the sons of God presented themselves before the Lord. And again the Lord said to Satan, "Have you seen my servant Job, that there is none like him in the earth? He is a perfect man. After all you have done to him, he has not changed."

Satan replied, "A man will give all he has to save his life. Put forth your hand now and touch his bone and his flesh. He will then curse you to your face."

The Lord said, "He is in your power. But save his life."

So Satan went forth and gave Job terrible boils from the soles of his feet to the top of his head.

Job's wife said to him, "After all this, do you still love God? Curse God, and die."

Job replied, "You speak like one of the foolish women. Shall we take good things from God and never evil?"

Job's friend Eliphaz said to Job, "Who ever perished that was innocent? Happy is the man whom God corrects."

"I have done no wrong," Job answered. "You would know if I lied."

Another friend, Bildad, said, "How long will you say things like that? If you were pure and upright, surely God would bless you."

"God takes things away, and who can stop him?" Job answered. "Who will say to God, 'What are you doing?' I will not say to God, 'Do not condemn me.'"

Still a third friend, Zophar, said, "You say, 'I have done no wrong.' But God is punishing you less than your sin deserves."

Job answered, "What miserable comforters you are! If you were in my place, I would strengthen and comfort you with my words."

But still Job's friends continued to say he must repent.

Job asked them, "How long will you vex my soul with your words? Why are you so cruel to me? I know that my Redeemer lives. He will stand on the earth in the last days. And though after I die, worms destroy this body, yet in my flesh I shall see God."

Still Eliphaz insisted, "Is not your wickedness great?"

Job replied, "After God has tried me, I shall come forth as gold."

No matter what Job said or did, his friends would not listen. Finally the Lord spoke to Eliphaz. "I am angry with you and your two friends," he said. "You have not spoken right as my servant Job has. So take seven young bulls and seven rams. Go to my servant Job and offer up a burnt offering."

After this warning, Eliphaz, Bildad, and Zophar repented. They did as the Lord commanded.

At last Job's time of testing was over. He had been valiant even in times of great trouble. Because of this, the Lord gave him seven more sons, three more daughters, and twice as much wealth as he had before.

—

JOB 1–42

DANIEL IN BABYLON

When Judah was captured by Babylon, the smartest and most talented Israelites were taken to Babylon. In Babylon they lived in King Nebuchadnezzar's palace. The king fed them the best foods. He also had them taught all the knowledge of that day.

Four of these young men were Daniel, Hananiah, Mishael, and Azariah. To show they had a new master, Nebuchadnezzar gave them new names. Daniel became Belteshazzar. Hananiah became Shadrach. Mishael became Meshach and Azariah became Abed-nego.

Daniel and his friends lived the Word of Wisdom of that time. They did not want to eat the unclean meat and wine that the king gave them. They asked for water and foods made of

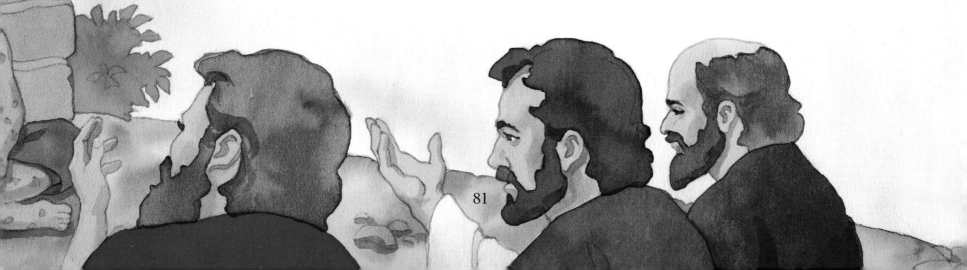

grain. This worried the servant. He was afraid that such foods would make the young men weak. Then the king would be displeased.

"Test us for ten days," Daniel begged the servant. "After that, compare us to those who eat the king's food."

For the next ten days the boys ate the foods they wanted. At the end of ten days, they were healthier than those who ate the king's food.

Because of their obedience, God gave the boys great knowledge and skill. At the end of their training, all the young men were presented to the king. Nebuchadnezzar questioned each one. Daniel, Shadrach, Meshach, and Abed-nego knew ten times more than all the wise men of the kingdom. Thus Daniel and his friends found favor with the king.

—

DANIEL 1

IN THE FIERY FURNACE

King Nebuchadnezzar made an idol out of gold. It stood ninety feet high and was nine feet wide. When it was finished, he sent for all the important men of the country. The king told the men that music would be played. Then they were to fall down and worship the idol. Those who would not worship would be cast into a furnace of fire.

Soon music filled the air. At its sound the men bowed. But Shadrach, Meshach, and Abed-nego did not bow. Because they would not worship the false god, they were taken to the king.

"Is it true?" the king asked. "Do you not worship the golden image?"

Shadrach, Meshach, and Abed-nego told him, "We will not serve your gods. We will not worship a golden image."

This made Nebuchadnezzar angry. He commanded the furnace to be heated seven times hotter than usual. He ordered his soldiers to throw Shadrach, Meshach, and Abed-nego into the fire.

The soldiers bound Shadrach, Meshach, and Abed-nego. They carried them to the furnace and threw them in. The fire was so hot it killed the soldiers. But Shadrach, Meshach, and Abed-nego were not hurt.

The king was amazed. He leaped forward to look closer. "Did we not cast three men into the fire?" he asked.

"True, O king," his servants answered.

"I see four men walking in the fire. They are not hurt. The fourth is like the Son of God!"

The king went to the mouth of the burning furnace. "Shadrach, Meshach, and Abed-nego," he called, "servants of the most high God, come forth."

The three climbed out. But not a hair of their heads was singed or their coats burned. They didn't even smell like fire.

"Blessed be the God of Shadrach, Meshach, and Abed-nego," Nebuchadnezzar said. "He has delivered his servants that trusted in him. No other God can do such a thing."

—

DANIEL 3

When Darius became king of Babylon, he appointed 120 princes to rule over the kingdom. Over the princes were three presidents. Daniel was the first president. But the other princes were jealous of Daniel. They made a plan to ruin him.

The princes went to the king. They told him, "You are so great, you are like a god. We think you should make a law that says no man shall pray to anyone except you for thirty days. If anyone does not obey, he shall be cast into a den of lions."

King Darius liked their idea. He made the law.

Now, Daniel knew of the law, but he loved God more than any man. So three times a day, he went into his house, knelt by a window, and prayed. This was exactly what the princes hoped. When they saw Daniel praying to God, they hurried to tell the king.

The princes said to the king, "Daniel disobeys your law. He still prays three times a day to his God."

King Darius was unhappy when he heard this. He loved Daniel very much and did not want to throw him to the lions. But the men insisted. They said, "Remember, O king, that no law of the king may be changed."

The king was trapped by his own law. So he had Daniel cast into the den of lions. But he said to Daniel, "Your God will save you."

Then he left Daniel alone with the hungry lions.

All that night the king fasted. He was so worried about Daniel that he could not sleep. Early the next morning, he ran to the lions' den. He cried out, "Daniel, O Daniel! Has your God saved you from the lions?"

Daniel answered, "O king, live forever. My God has sent his angel and has shut the lions' mouths. They have not hurt me."

The king was very glad. He had Daniel taken out of the den. Then he had the men who accused Daniel cast into the lions' den.

After this King Darius sent a message to all the people of his kingdom. It said, "I make a law that in all my kingdom men should fear the God of Daniel, for he is the living God."

—

DANIEL 6

JONAH AND THE GREAT FISH

One day, the Lord spoke to the prophet Jonah. He said, "Go to Nineveh and tell the people to repent, for I have seen their wickedness."

But Jonah was afraid to go to Nineveh. Instead, he got on a ship going to Tarshish. Tarshish was far away from Nineveh.

But Jonah could not run away from the Lord. As the ship set out to sea, the Lord sent a great storm. The wind beat against the ship so hard the sailors thought it would break. They threw out their belongings into the water to make the ship lighter. But that did not help.

Jonah was asleep inside the ship. He didn't even know about the storm. When the shipmaster found Jonah, he woke him. "Why are you sleeping?" he asked. "Get up and pray to your God so that we will not die!"

But the storm went on. The sailors cast lots to find out who was causing this trouble. The lot fell upon Jonah.

The men asked Jonah, "What work do you do? Where do you come from?"

Jonah answered, "I am a Hebrew. I fear the Lord who has made the sea and the dry land." Then he told them how he had come to be on the ship.

When the sailors knew Jonah had fled from the Lord, they were even more afraid. "Why have you done this?" they asked. "What shall we do with you now?"

Jonah replied, "Throw me into the sea. Then the sea will be calm. For I know it is because of me that this great storm has come."

The men did not want to hurt Jonah. They rowed hard and tried to bring the ship to land, but they couldn't. Not knowing what else to do, they finally threw Jonah into the raging sea. As soon as they did, the storm stopped.

As for Jonah, the Lord sent a great fish to swallow him. Jonah stayed in the belly of the fish for three days and three nights. While he was there, he prayed to the Lord. He repented of the wrong he had done in not going to Nineveh. After Jonah repented, the Lord spoke to the fish. It spit Jonah out onto the dry land.

Again the Lord said to Jonah, "Go to Nineveh and preach to the people."

This time Jonah obeyed. He went to Nineveh and preached the word of the Lord. To his surprise the people listened and believed. To show their repentance, they fasted and put on sackcloth. Even the king arose from his throne, covered himself with sackcloth, and sat in ashes. Because of this, the judgments of God did not fall upon the people of Nineveh.

—

JONAH 1–4

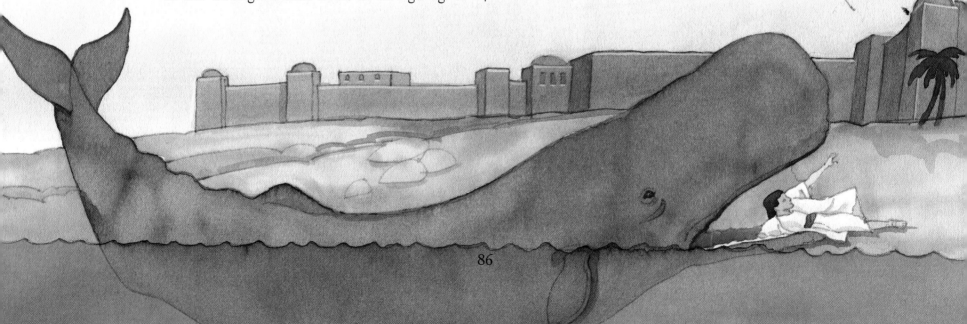

Zacharias and Elisabeth lived in the days of Herod the Great, the governor of Judea. They had been married many years but had no children. This caused them great sorrow. However, they loved the Lord and trusted in his wisdom.

Now in that day there were twenty-four orders of priests. The orders of priests took turns serving in the temple. However, there were thousands of priests in each order. Because of this, the chance to serve in the temple was rare. But when the week came for the order of Abia to serve, Zacharias was chosen.

Each morning of the week of his service, Zacharias climbed the steps to the temple. While he entered the temple, the people waited outside. Alone he walked to the altar that stood before the veil. On the altar he lighted the incense.

One day as he was lighting the incense, the angel Gabriel appeared. When Gabriel lived on the earth, he was called Noah. "Fear not, Zacharias," Gabriel said. "I am sent to give you good news. Your prayer is heard. Your wife Elisabeth shall bear a son."

Zacharias was amazed. But he listened to what Gabriel said. "You shall call the baby John. He shall drink no wine or strong drink. He shall be filled with the Holy Ghost, even before he is born. He will prepare a people for the Lord."

"How shall I know this is true?" Zacharias asked. "I am an old man. My wife is also old."

"You shall not be able to speak until after the baby is born," Gabriel answered.

Outside the people began to worry. Why was Zacharias taking so long? When he finally came out, the people were more amazed. Zacharias could not speak!

Just as the angel promised, Elisabeth had a son. Friends and family were happy for Elisabeth and Zacharias. When he was eight days old, they went to the temple to circumcise the baby. The people called the baby Zacharias. But Elisabeth said, "No, his name is John."

"No one in your family is called John," they said. Then they made signs to Zacharias to see what name he wanted.

On a tablet Zacharias wrote, "His name is John."

As soon as he wrote the words, Zacharias could speak. All who heard him remembered his words. They knew this baby would become a very special man.

—

LUKE 1

One day, the angel Gabriel came to a virgin named Mary, who lived in the city of Nazareth.

Gabriel said to Mary, "The Lord is with you. Blessed are you among women."

Mary was frightened. She wondered what the angel meant.

Gabriel said to her, "Fear not, Mary, for you have found favor with God. You shall have a son and shall call his name Jesus. He shall be great. He will reign over the house of Jacob forever."

Mary asked, "How shall this be?"

The angel replied, "The child you shall bear will be called the Son of God. Behold, your cousin Elisabeth has also conceived a son. For with God nothing is impossible."

Mary then said, "Behold the handmaid of the Lord. Be it unto me according to your word."

At these words, Gabriel left her.

Mary was betrothed to Joseph. When Joseph learned that Mary was going to have a child, he was worried about what he should do. Then one day Gabriel appeared to Joseph.

Gabriel said to him, "Joseph, son of David, fear not to take Mary as your wife, for the baby she will have is of the Holy Ghost. She shall bring forth a son, and you shall call his name

Jesus, for he shall save his people from their sins."

So Mary and Joseph were married.

Soon after, the Roman emperor, Caesar Augustus, sent out a decree that everyone in his empire should be taxed. All the men had to go to the town where they were born and put their names on

the tax roll. Joseph had to go to Bethlehem, a town about seventy miles south of Nazareth. Joseph took Mary with him.

When they arrived in Bethlehem, the city was filled with people. All of the inns were full. But one innkeeper had a stable where he said Mary and Joseph could stay. There Jesus was born. Mary wrapped the baby in swaddling clothes and laid him in a feeding trough called a manger.

Nearby, shepherds were watching over their sheep in a field. An angel of the Lord suddenly appeared to them. The shepherds were frightened.

"Fear not!" the angel said. "I bring you good tidings of great joy, which shall be to all people. For unto you is born this day, in the city of David, a Savior, who is Christ the Lord. This shall be a sign unto you. You shall find the babe wrapped in swaddling clothes and lying in a manger."

Then the angel was joined by a great choir of angels. "Glory to God in the highest," they sang. "And on earth peace, goodwill toward men."

After the angels left, the shepherds looked at one another in amazement. "Let us go and see this thing which the Lord has made known to us," they said. They hurried to Bethlehem, where they found Mary and Joseph and the babe lying in a manger.

Afterward the shepherds returned and thanked God for what they had heard and seen. They told others that the Savior had at last been born.

When Jesus was eight days old, Mary and Joseph took him to the temple in Jerusalem to be circumcised. That day, the Holy Ghost prompted a man named Simeon to go to the temple. He was an old man, and the Holy Ghost had promised him that he would not die until he had seen the Savior. When Mary and Joseph arrived at the temple, Simeon saw the baby and took him in his arms. "Lord, now let your servant depart in peace," he said, "for my eyes have seen your salvation."

A prophetess named Anna was also in the temple that day. She was an old widow who stayed in the temple fasting and praying and serving God. When she saw the baby, she also gave thanks to the Lord. Then she, too, bore testimony that the Savior had come.

Later wise men from the east came to Jerusalem. They went to King Herod and asked, "Where is the child that is born King of the Jews? We have seen his star in the east and are come to worship him."

This worried Herod. He was king, and he did not want anyone taking his place. He gathered his scribes and priests and asked them where Christ would be born. They answered, "The prophets have written that he will be born in Bethlehem of Judea."

King Herod then called the wise men to him. "Go and search for the young child," he said. "When you have found him, bring me word, so I may worship him also."

But Herod was lying. He did not want to worship Jesus; he wanted to kill him.

The wise men left Herod and followed the star to Bethlehem. When they went into the house where Jesus was, they saw Mary holding the baby, and bowed down. They worshipped this baby that they knew was their Savior. Then they gave him gifts of gold, frankincense, and myrrh.

The wise men remembered that King Herod had told them to tell him when they found Jesus. But God warned them in a dream not to tell Herod. Instead, they returned to their own country.

After the wise men left, an angel came to Joseph in a dream. "Arise," the angel said. "Take the child and his mother and flee into Egypt. Stay there until I bring you word. For Herod will seek to destroy the child."

So Joseph took Mary and Jesus and went to Egypt.

When the wise men did not return, Herod was angry. He wanted to make sure no child grew up to take his place as king. So he ordered all children under two years of age to be killed.

Because an angel had told Joseph to take Mary and Jesus to Egypt, Jesus was safe. But John was still living in Judea. Zacharias told Elisabeth to take John into the wilderness. There she cared for him and fed him locust and wild honey. However, Zacharias was now the officiating high priest in the temple. He stayed in Jerusalem to complete his service.

One day soldiers marched into the temple. They demanded that Zacharias tell them where John was hiding. When Zacharias refused, the soldiers killed him as he stood between the porch and the altar.

In the wilderness, John grew to be a strong man. He was baptized, and the Lord taught him. Thus he was also strong in spirit.

—

MATTHEW 1–2; LUKE 1–2
(SEE ALSO *TEACHINGS OF
THE PROPHET JOSEPH SMITH*, 261;
D&C 84:28)

When Herod the Great died, an angel was sent to Joseph in Egypt. "Take the child and his mother back to Israel," the angel said. "They are dead who sought to kill the child."

So Joseph took Mary and Jesus home to Nazareth. There Jesus grew up with sisters and four brothers. The brothers were named James, Joses, Simon, and Judas. Joseph taught Jesus to be a carpenter. God taught Jesus to be the Messiah.

Each year Mary and Joseph went to Jerusalem for the Passover. In Jerusalem they worshipped and ate the Passover Feast with family and friends. The year Jesus was twelve years old, he also went. When the feast was over, Mary and Joseph began the trip home. Many people were traveling together, and Mary thought Jesus was with them. But when they stopped, Mary could not find Jesus.

Mary and Joseph hurried back to Jerusalem. They searched the narrow streets and crowded marketplaces for three days. But they could not find Jesus. Then Mary found him in the temple. He was sitting with the priests and teachers. He was listening, asking questions, and teaching. All who heard Jesus were amazed at his understanding.

"Son, why have you done this?" Mary asked. "Joseph and I have been filled with worry."

"Do you not know that I must be about my Father's business?" Jesus asked.

Then Jesus returned with them to Nazareth. There he lived with his family until it was time for his work to begin.

—

LUKE 2;
JST MATTHEW 3:24–26;
MATTHEW 13:55

When Jesus was about thirty years old, God told John it was time to teach the Jews. John said to them, "Repent, for the kingdom of heaven is at hand!"

People from all parts of Judea went out to hear John. Those who believed his words were baptized.

One day while John was preaching beside the River Jordan, Jesus came to him. He wanted to be baptized. At first John refused. He said, "I need to be baptized by you. Why do you come to me?"

Jesus said, "Let me be baptized. It is necessary in order to fulfill all righteousness."

So John took Jesus into the River Jordan and baptized him. As Jesus came out of the water, the heavens opened, and the Holy Ghost came down and lighted upon Jesus. A voice from heaven said, "This is my beloved Son, in whom I am well pleased."

After Jesus was baptized, the Holy Ghost led him into the wilderness. There he fasted and prayed for forty days and forty nights. While he was there, angels taught him.

At the end of the forty days, Jesus was very hungry. Knowing this, Satan came to him. Satan said, "If you are the Son of God, command that these stones become bread."

But Jesus answered, "It is written, 'Man shall not live by bread alone, but by every word that proceeds from the mouth of God.'"

Then the Holy Ghost took Jesus to the temple in Jerusalem. While he was standing on the highest pinnacle of the temple, Satan came to him again. Satan said, "Throw yourself down from here. If you are the Son of God, angels will catch you so you are not hurt."

But Jesus answered, "It is written again, 'You shall not tempt the Lord your God.'"

Then the Holy Ghost took Jesus to a high mountain and showed him all the kingdoms of the world and their glory. Again Satan came to him and said, "All this will I give you, if you will fall down and worship me."

But Jesus answered, "Get away from me, Satan, for it is written, 'You shall worship the Lord your God, and him only shall you serve.'"

Defeated, Satan left for a time. When he was gone, the angels came again to visit with Jesus.

—

JST MATTHEW 3–4;
MARK 1; LUKE 4

After he was baptized, Jesus went about the land preaching. One day he climbed a hill and began to teach.

"Blessed are they who believe on me and are baptized. They shall be visited by the Holy Ghost," Jesus said. "They shall be forgiven of their sins.

"And blessed are the poor in spirit who come to me. Theirs is the kingdom of heaven.

"Blessed are they that mourn. They shall be comforted.

"Blessed are the meek. They shall inherit the earth."

The people listened as Jesus told them more. "Blessed are all they who hunger and thirst after righteousness. They shall be filled with the Holy Ghost.

"And blessed are the merciful. They shall obtain mercy.

"Blessed are the pure in heart. They shall see God.

"Blessed are the peacemakers. They shall be called the children of God. And blessed are they who are hurt for my sake. Theirs is the kingdom of heaven.

"Blessed are you when men speak falsely against you for my sake. You shall have great joy and be glad. Great shall be your reward in heaven."

These sayings are called the Beatitudes. After teaching the Beatitudes, Jesus told them many other things. He taught them to be an example to the world. He taught them to be peacemakers. He taught them to keep their language clean and to forgive others. He also taught them to love even their enemies.

After he taught these things, he told them to pray and to seek the kingdom of God. If they did this, he promised that everything else they needed would be given to them.

—

MATTHEW 5–7; JST MATTHEW 5–7;
3 NEPHI 12

One day, Jesus asked his apostles to take him to the other side of the Sea of Galilee in a boat. When he got into the boat, he lay down. The gentle sway of the water soon rocked him to sleep.

As they sailed, a great storm arose. The waves were so high they covered the boat and tossed it upon the sea. Still, Jesus slept.

The apostles were frightened. They woke up Jesus and said, "Lord, save us, for we perish!"

Jesus asked them, "Why are you fearful?"

Then he arose and commanded the winds and water to be still. Immediately a great calm fell over the sea.

The men on the boat marveled. They said, "What manner of man is this, that even the winds and the sea obey him?"

When he returned to his own city, Jesus was walking through the streets of the city. A woman who suffered from a terrible blood disease saw him. She had spent twelve years and much money seeking a cure for her sickness. But instead of getting better, she grew sicker.

She had heard the teachings of Jesus. She believed his words. She knew that he had power to heal her. So when she saw him, she touched the hem of his cloak. Immediately she was healed.

Jesus felt the healing power go from him and stopped. "Who touched my clothes?" he asked.

The disciples were amazed. "There are hundreds of people touching you," they said. "How can you ask, 'Who touched me?'"

Then Jesus turned. The woman was afraid. She thought she had done something wrong. She bowed and told Jesus what she had done.

"Daughter, be comforted," Jesus said. "Your faith has made you whole. Go in peace."

—

MATTHEW 8–9;
JST MATTHEW 8; MARK 5;
JST MARK 5; LUKE 8

One time while Jesus was teaching, a lawyer asked him, "Master, what shall I do to inherit eternal life?"

Jesus answered, "Love the Lord with all your heart, with all your soul, with all your strength, and with all your mind. And love your neighbor as yourself."

The lawyer then asked, "Who is my neighbor?"

Jesus answered with this parable:

A certain man was traveling from Jerusalem to Jericho. Along the way, he was attacked by thieves. The thieves wounded him, took his money and clothes, and left him for dead.

Soon after, a priest passed by. When he saw the wounded man, he crossed to the other side of the road and hurried on his way. A Levite also came by. When he saw the man, he too crossed to the other side of the road and hurried on. But a Samaritan saw the wounded man and had compassion on him. He bound up the man's wounds, put him on his own beast, and took him to an inn. There he cared for him.

The next day, when it was time for the Samaritan to leave, he gave the innkeeper some money. He said to the innkeeper, "Take care of him. Whatever more you spend, I will repay you when I come again."

After he told the story, Jesus asked the lawyer, "Now, which of these three do you think was neighbor to the man that fell among the thieves?"

The lawyer answered, "He that showed mercy on him."

Jesus said, "Go, and do likewise."

—

LUKE 10

95

Jesus taught another parable.

A certain man had two sons. One day the youngest said to him, "Father, give me my share of your wealth now." So the father gave him his share. The son then left home and went to another country to live. There he wasted his money on pleasures and wild living. By the time his money was gone, a famine came to the land. The young man was hungry and homeless. He found a job feeding pigs. But he was still so hungry he wished he could eat the pigs' food.

Then one day he thought, "The servants of my father have bread while I perish with hunger. I will go to my father. I will say to him, 'Father, I have sinned against heaven and against you. I am not worthy to be called your son. But make me one of your servants.'" So he went toward home.

When he was still a long way off, his father saw him coming. He ran to meet him. He hugged and kissed his son. The son said, "Father, I have sinned against heaven and against you. I am not worthy to be called your son."

But the father said to his servants, "Bring the best robe and put it on him. Put a ring on his hand. Put shoes on his feet. Then kill a calf and let us eat and be merry, for this my son was dead and is alive again. He was lost and is found."

And all began to be merry.

The older brother had been working in the fields. When he came home, he heard the music and excitement. He asked what was happening. One of the servants said, "Your brother is home. Your father is holding a feast to celebrate."

When the older brother heard this, he was angry. He refused to go in. His father went out to see what was wrong.

The older son said, "All these years I have worked for you. I have never disobeyed you. But you never gave me a feast. Yet as soon as this son came, who has spent his money on evil, you prepared a feast."

The father answered, "Son, you are always with me. All that I have is yours. But it is right for us to make merry and be glad, for your brother was lost and is now found."

—

LUKE 15

Herod Antipas, one of the sons of Herod the Great, was now the ruler in Galilee. Like his father, he was a selfish, wicked man. He fell in love with Herodias, his brother's wife, and married her.

John did not approve of such wickedness. "It is not lawful for you to marry your brother's wife," he told Herod.

This made Herod very angry. He ordered his soldiers to throw John into prison. He wanted to kill John. But Herod knew the people considered John a prophet. Because of this, he was afraid to kill John.

When Jesus heard that his cousin was in prison, he sent angels to minister unto John.

After some time Herod Antipas held a great feast to celebrate his birthday. At the feast Herodias's daughter Salome danced. Salome was very beautiful. She pleased Herod very much. When the dance ended, Herod said, "Whatever you ask of me, I will give it to you."

Salome did not know what to ask for. She hurried to her mother. "What should I ask?"

Herodias hated John, so she said, "Ask for the head of John the Baptist."

Salome went back to Herod. "I want the head of John the Baptist," she said.

Herod was sorry that he had given Salome the promise. If he killed John, the people might rise up against him. But he did not want to look like a coward. So he ordered John's death. Soon a servant returned with John's head on a charger and presented it to Salome.

When the disciples heard what had happened, they were sad. They put John's body in a tomb, and then hurried to tell Jesus the awful news.

—

MATTHEW 14; MARK 6

JESUS FEEDS FIVE THOUSAND PEOPLE

When Jesus heard that Herod had killed John, he was very sad. Taking his apostles in a boat, he crossed the Sea of Galilee. There he found a place where he could be alone. But the people found where he had gone and followed.

When they came, Jesus taught them and healed them. But evening soon came and the people were hungry. Jesus' apostles came to him and said, "Send the multitude away, for there is nothing here for them to eat."

But Jesus said to them, "They need not go away. Give them food to eat."

The apostles asked, "Shall we go and buy bread?"

Jesus said, "How many loaves do the people have? Go and see."

Soon they returned. "There is a boy here who has five loaves and two small fishes. But what is that among so many people?"

Jesus said, "Ask the people to sit on the grass."

When the people were all seated, Jesus took the five loaves and the two fishes. Looking up to heaven, he blessed the food. After it was blessed, he broke the loaves and gave them to his apostles. He told them to feed the people.

Now, there were about five thousand men with their women and children. But everyone ate until he or she was full. When they were through eating, Jesus told the apostles to gather up the food that was left. When they brought the leftovers to Jesus, there were twelve baskets filled with food.

The people said, "This is truly the promised prophet."

Many of them said, "We should make him king!"

This displeased Jesus greatly. He told the apostles to take the boat across the sea. He promised to meet them later. After they were gone, he sent the people away. Alone at last, he climbed the mountainside and prayed.

—

MATTHEW 14;
MARK 6;
LUKE 9;
JOHN 6

As the apostles sailed upon the Sea of Galilee, a terrible wind came up. It was blowing in the wrong direction. The apostles took down the sail and rowed against the wind. They rowed through the night but made no progress. They grew tired and feared for their lives.

Then they looked out over the rolling sea and saw a man walking toward them on the water.

They cried out in fear, "It is a spirit!"

But it was Jesus. He called out to them, "Be of good cheer! It is I. Be not afraid."

Peter called back, "Lord, if it is you, ask me to come to you on the water!"

"Come," Jesus answered.

Eagerly, Peter climbed out of the boat, stepped onto the water, and began to walk toward Jesus. But as he walked, he looked at the great waves and felt the wind whipping his cloak. Suddenly his mind filled with doubt and fear, and he fell into the water.

He cried, "Lord, save me!"

Jesus stretched forth his hand and caught hold of Peter. "Why did you doubt?" he asked.

The apostles helped Jesus and Peter into the boat. As soon as they were in, the wind stopped.

The apostles were amazed. They worshipped Jesus, saying, "Truly, you are the Son of God."

—

MATTHEW 14;
MARK 6; JOHN 6

THE BLIND CAN SEE

One Sabbath day Jesus was walking through the streets of Jerusalem with his disciples. He saw a man who had been blind from birth. As they passed the man, the disciples asked, "Master, who sinned and caused him to be born blind, this man or his parents?"

Jesus answered, "Neither. He is blind so that the works of God can be shown in him."

Jesus went on to say, "I must work the works of him that sent me, while it is day. The night comes, when no man can work. As long as I am in the world, I am the light of the world."

Then Jesus spit on the ground and made clay. He put the clay on the eyes of the blind man. "Go, wash in the pool of Siloam," he said.

The man went to the pool and washed the clay from his eyes. To his great joy, he could see!

—
JOHN 9:1–7

JESUS BRINGS LAZARUS BACK FROM DEATH

Jesus had a friend named Lazarus who lived in Bethany. Lazarus became very ill. His sisters, Mary and Martha, sent a message to Jesus: "Lord, he whom you love is sick."

When Jesus got the message, he said to his apostles, "This sickness is for the glory of God and the Son of God."

Jesus waited two more days. Then he said to his apostles, "Let us go to Judea again. Our friend Lazarus sleeps. I go to wake him."

Jesus meant that Lazarus had died. The apostles did not understand. They said, "Lord, if he sleeps, he will get well."

Then Jesus told them, "Lazarus is dead. I am glad for your sakes that I was not there. I want you to believe. Let us go to him."

When Jesus arrived in Bethany, Lazarus had been dead for four days. His body had been placed in a cave and a big rock had been rolled over the opening. Many people had gathered to comfort Martha and Mary as they grieved for their brother.

When Martha heard that Jesus was coming, she ran to greet him.

Mary cried, "Lord, if you had been here, my brother would not have died. But I know that even now, God will give you whatever you ask."

Jesus said, "Your brother shall rise again."

Martha answered, "I know he shall rise again in the resurrection."

Jesus said, "I am the resurrection, and the life. He that believes in me, though he were dead, yet shall he live. And whoever lives and believes in me shall never die. Do you believe this?"

Mary answered, "Yes, Lord. I believe you are the Christ, the Son of God."

Then Martha went back to Mary. She said, "The Master is coming and calls for you."

Mary ran quickly from the house. The people said, "She goes to the grave to weep."

They followed her. But instead, Mary ran to greet Jesus. When she neared Jesus, Mary fell down at his feet. She said, "Lord, if you had been here, my brother would not have died."

Jesus asked, "Where have they laid him?"

The people answered, "Lord, come and see."

Seeing Mary and the others weeping, Jesus also wept.

"See how he loved Lazarus!" some people said.

But others said, "This man opened the eyes of the blind. Could he not have kept this man from dying?"

Jesus knew what they were saying, and he was troubled.

When they came to the tomb, Jesus said, "Take away the stone."

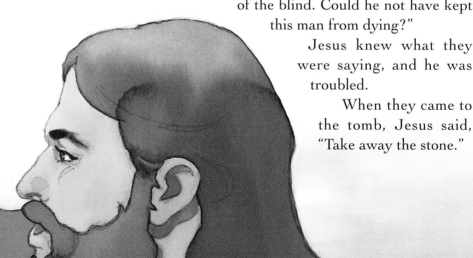

101

Mary said, "Lord, by this time he stinks. He has been dead four days."

Jesus answered, "Did not I say to you that if you would believe, you would see the glory of God?"

So the people moved the rock away from the opening of the tomb. Then Jesus, lifting up his eyes, said, "Father, I thank you that you have heard me. I know that you always hear me. But I said it so that these people may hear and believe that you have sent me."

Then Jesus cried with a loud voice, "Lazarus, come forth!"

And Lazarus walked out of the tomb. His hands and feet were still wrapped with grave clothes. His face was covered with a napkin.

Jesus said, "Unwrap him, and let him go."

Thus Lazarus was reunited with Martha and Mary.

Now, many of the Jews who saw this miracle believed in Jesus. But not all believed. Some of them only hated him more, and they tried all the harder to take his life.

—

JOHN 11

A ROYAL ARRIVAL

One Sunday morning, Jesus and his disciples walked to Jerusalem. When they reached the Mount of Olives, Jesus stopped. "Go into the village of Bethphage," he told two of his disciples. "When you have entered, you shall find a donkey and her colt. Untie them and bring them to me. If any man asks why you are taking the animals, say the Lord needs them. Then he will send them."

Now all this was according to the prophecy

made many years before. "Fear not, daughter of Zion," Zacharias had said. "Your king comes to you. He is meek. He is sitting upon a donkey, and a colt."

The disciples went into Jerusalem. They found the donkey and colt. Just as Jesus told them, the animals were tied near a door

in a place where two streets met. They began to untie the animals.

"Why are you untying the colt?" some men asked.

"Because the Lord has need of him," the disciples answered. When the men heard that it was Jesus who needed them, they let the animals go.

The disciples returned to Jesus. They spread their cloaks upon the colt's back. Jesus then sat upon the colt, and they went back to Jerusalem. The disciples began to rejoice and to shout praises to God. People heard the noise. They ran from their houses and shops.

When they saw Jesus coming, they joined the disciples. They cast their cloaks upon the

ground to make a path for Jesus. Some people cut branches from palm trees and waved them in the air. Others added the branches to the path of cloaks.

Some of the Pharisees were also in the crowd. They heard the shouting. They saw how the people honored Jesus. They said, "Master, rebuke your disciples."

"If they hold their peace, the stones will cry out," Jesus answered.

Jesus rode through the streets until he came to the temple. He got off the colt and entered the temple. There he blessed his disciples and taught them. When evening arrived, he went to Bethany.

The next morning, Jesus again went to the temple. Already the temple was filled with money changers and men who sold animals for offerings. These men had not come to the temple to worship. They came to make money. They shouted and argued as they went about their business.

"My house shall be called the house of prayer," Jesus told them. "But you have made it a den of thieves!" Then he threw over the tables and seats.

When the money changers were gone, Jesus began to teach the people. The priests and scribes watched. They knew the people loved Jesus very much. They were jealous. Their jealousy kept them from hearing his message of love. They could only think about their wealth and authority being lost. They would not let such a thing happen. From that moment on, they sought for a way to kill Jesus.

—
MATTHEW 21; MARK 11;
LUKE 19; JOHN 12

THE LAST SUPPER

On the first day of Passover, the apostles asked Jesus, "Where do you want us to eat the Passover?"

Jesus said to Peter and John, "Go into the city. There you will meet a man carrying a pitcher of water. Follow him. Where he goes in, say to the man of the house, 'The Master says, Where is the room in which I shall eat the Passover with my disciples?' He will show you a large upper room. Make it ready for us."

When the evening of the Passover came, Jesus and the twelve apostles gathered in the upper room. Jesus said to them, "I want to eat this Passover meal with you before I suffer."

As they were eating, Jesus stood and took off his cloak. He wrapped a towel around his waist. Then he poured water into a basin. Taking the water, he began to wash the feet of each of the disciples. When it came Peter's turn, Peter said, "Lord, do you wash my feet?"

Jesus answered, "You don't know now what I am doing. But you will understand later."

Peter said, "You don't need to wash my feet."

Jesus answered, "If I wash you not, you will have no part with me."

Peter said to him, "Then, Lord, wash not only my feet, but also my hands and my head."

Jesus answered, "He that has washed his hands and his head needs only to wash his feet to be clean. But you are not all clean." Now, Jesus said this because he knew that Judas was plotting to betray him. But the other apostles did not know what Jesus meant.

After Jesus finished washing their feet, he put on his cloak. "Do you know what I have done to you?" he asked. "You call me Master and Lord, and that is good, for so I am. But if I, your Lord and Master, have washed your feet, you also ought to wash one another's feet. I have given you an example, that you should do as I have done to you."

As the apostles listened, Jesus went on teaching, "Verily, verily, I say unto you, the servant is not greater than his lord. If you know these things, happy are you if you do them."

After Jesus had said these words, he was troubled. He said, "Verily, verily, I say unto you, that one of you shall betray me."

The apostles could hardly believe these words. They looked at one another. They loved the Lord. How could one of them who had seen so many miracles and heard his marvelous teachings betray him? Surely they had misunderstood!

John was sitting next to Jesus. He asked, "Lord, who is it?"

Jesus answered, "It is he to whom I shall give a sop when I have dipped it."

John watched as Jesus dipped the sop in a dish and handed it to Judas Iscariot.

"What you do, do quickly," Jesus said to Judas.

The other apostles did not understand why Jesus said this. They knew that Judas kept the money. They thought Jesus wanted him to go buy something or perhaps give something to the poor. But Judas knew what Jesus meant. He left and went out into the night.

After Judas was gone, Jesus told of his coming death. He told the apostles to carry on his work. He taught them about his resurrection and the Holy Ghost. He taught them about love.

He said, "A new commandment I give unto you, that you love one another. As I have loved you, you also should love one another. If you love one another, all men shall know that you are my disciples."

Then Jesus took bread, blessed it, broke it, and gave it to the disciples. "Take, eat," he commanded. "This is in remembrance of my body, which I give as a ransom for you."

Then he took a cup of wine, blessed it, and gave it to them. "Drink," he said, "for this is in remembrance of my blood. It is shed for as many as shall believe on my name for the remission of their sins. And I give unto you a commandment, that you shall do the things which you have seen me do, and bear record of me even unto the end."

Then Jesus said, "This night all of you shall be offended because of me."

Peter answered, "All men may be offended, yet I will never be offended."

"Verily, I say unto you, Peter, this night, before the cock crows, you shall deny me three times," said Jesus.

Peter said, "Even if I should die with you, I would not deny you."

Jesus went on teaching. He said, "In my Father's house are many mansions. I go to prepare a place for you."

When Thomas heard this, he said, "Lord, we know not where you are going. How can we know the way?"

Jesus answered, "I am the way, the truth, and the life. No man cometh unto the Father but by me."

After the apostles asked a few more questions, Jesus said, "Verily, verily, I say unto you, he that believes on me, shall do the works that I do. And greater works than these shall he do, because I go unto my Father. If you love me, keep my commandments."

Jesus then said he would send another Comforter to stay with them. This Comforter was the Holy Ghost. It would teach and guide his people after he was gone.

When Jesus finished speaking, they sang a hymn and walked together to the Mount of Olives.

—

MATTHEW 26; JST MATTHEW 26; MARK 14; LUKE 22; JOHN 13; JST JOHN 13

IN GETHSEMANE

While the apostles walked with Jesus through the dark streets of Jerusalem, he continued to teach them. He said to them, "As the Father has loved me, so have I loved you. Continue in my love. If you keep my commandments, you shall abide in my love. This is my commandment, that you love one another as I have loved you."

The disciples asked questions, and Jesus answered. Then he said, "In the world you shall have tribulation, but be of good cheer. I have overcome the world."

Jesus then lifted his eyes to heaven and began to pray: "Father, the hour is come. Glorify your Son that your Son also may glorify you. You have given him power over all flesh that he should give eternal life to as many as follow him. And this is life eternal, that they might know you, the only true God, and Jesus Christ, whom you have sent."

When Jesus was finished praying, he and his apostles crossed over the Brook Cedron and entered an olive grove called the Garden of Gethsemane. There Jesus left eight of the apostles. He said, "Sit here, while I go and pray."

Taking Peter, James, and John, he walked farther into the garden. "My soul is very sorrowful," he said, "even unto death."

Finally he stopped. He said to Peter, James, and John, "Wait here. Watch with me, and pray that you enter not into temptation."

Then Jesus walked about a stone's throw away. There he knelt on the ground and prayed: "O my Father, if it be possible, let this cup pass from me. Nevertheless, not my will, but yours be done."

After praying, Jesus arose and went back to where he had left Peter, James, and John. But they had fallen asleep. "Peter, could you not watch with me one hour?" he asked. "The spirit truly is ready, but the flesh is weak."

Then Jesus left them to pray again. "O my Father," he prayed, "if this cup may not pass from me, except I drink it, your will be done."

Again he returned to find his three friends asleep. This time he did not wake them. He let them sleep while he returned to pray for the third time.

During these prayers, in a way we do not fully understand, Jesus took upon himself the sins of all mankind. He suffered the torment, the sorrow, and the pain of those sins so that the law of justice could be fulfilled. The pain was so great that an angel came to comfort him. The pain caused Jesus to sweat great drops of blood. But Jesus endured it because he loved us so much.

When he finished praying the third time, Jesus returned to Peter, James, and John. "Sleep on now, and rest," he said. "For behold, the hour is at hand, and the Son of man is betrayed into the hands of sinners."

When they awoke, Jesus said, "Arise, and let us go. Behold, he is at hand that betrays me."

As Jesus spoke, Judas came with a great multitude. They were armed with swords and staves and carrying lanterns and torches. Among the multitude were many of the chief priests and the elders of the people. Judas had told them, "The man I kiss, that same is Jesus. Hold him fast."

As they came near, Judas stepped forward. "Hail, master," he said, and he kissed Jesus.

Jesus asked, "Judas, do you betray the Son of man with a kiss?" Then he stepped forward to face the multitude. "Whom do you seek?" he asked.

"Jesus of Nazareth," they answered.

Jesus said, "I am he."

The people were astonished and fell backward. Many even fell to the ground.

Jesus asked again, "Whom do you seek?"

Again they said, "Jesus of Nazareth."

Jesus said, "I have told you that I am he. If you are looking only for me, let my apostles go their way."

At these words the soldiers laid their hands on Jesus and bound him. Seeing what was happening, one of the apostles asked, "Shall we smite them with the sword?"

Simon Peter, who was holding a sword, did not wait for an answer. He quickly stretched out his hand and struck a man named Malchus with his sword. The blow cut off Malchus's right ear.

Jesus said, "Put away your sword, Peter. All they who take the sword shall perish with the sword. Do you think that I cannot pray to my Father, and he would give me more than twelve legions of angels? But then how would the scriptures be fulfilled?"

Jesus then turned to Malchus. He touched Malchus's ear, and it was healed.

But even this did not soften the hearts of the angry mob. Shouting and cursing they led Jesus away. The apostles fled.

—

MATTHEW 26; JST MATTHEW 26;
MARK 14; JOHN 18

Torches suddenly dotted the darkness. Voices filled the night air. A crowd stomped through the streets of Jerusalem. They were following the soldiers who had taken Jesus prisoner. Behind the mob, Peter and John watched to see what would happen.

Slowly they wound their way to the palace of Caiaphas. The people at the palace knew John and let him enter. He asked the woman who kept the door to let Peter in. The woman agreed. As Peter entered, she asked, "Are you also one of Jesus' disciples?"

"I am not," Peter answered.

Inside the courtyard, a fire of coal burned. Peter stood near it. A young girl also came to stand by the fire. "This man is one of Jesus' disciples," she told the others.

"I am not!" Peter answered and moved into the shadows.

A little later a servant came by. When he saw Peter, he said, "Did I not see you in the garden with Jesus?"

"No," Peter answered, and at that moment the cock crowed. At the sound, Peter remembered the words of Jesus: "Before the cock crows, you shall deny me three times." Filled with sorrow, Peter went out and cried bitterly.

In the Jewish law it was illegal to hold a trial at night. But the Jewish leaders held the trial anyway. And since Jesus had broken no law, they bribed witnesses to lie about him. But the stories were not the same. Thus no judgment could be passed.

Jesus listened to the false words. But he did not speak. Finally Caiaphas stood. "Answer you nothing?" he asked Jesus. "Do you not know what these men say against you?"

Still Jesus did not speak.

Then Caiaphas said, "Tell us whether you are the Christ, the Son of God. Tell us!"

"You have said," Jesus answered. "You shall see the Son of Man sitting on the right hand of God."

"He has spoken blasphemy!" the crowd cried. Then they put Jesus in prison until they could decide what to do.

While they waited, the soldiers began to mock Jesus. They put a blindfold over his eyes. They spit in his face. They slapped him with their hands. "If you are Christ," they said, "tell us who hit you!"

When Judas saw what was happening to Jesus, he took the thirty pieces of silver the chief priests had given him back to them. "I have sinned. I have betrayed innocent blood," Judas told them.

"What is that to us?" they asked.

Throwing the silver at their feet, Judas left.

He had done a terrible thing. He had betrayed the Son of God. He could not stop thinking about it. Hurrying away, Judas found a tree and hanged himself.

Day began to dawn. The Jewish leaders decided to take Jesus to the Roman governor of Judea. When they arrived at the hall of judgment, they would not enter. They thought it would make them unclean. So the governor, Pontius Pilate, came outside to meet them. They gave Jesus to Pilate.

Pilate said, "Judge the man according to your law."

"But it is not lawful for us to put a man to death," the priests answered.

Pilate did not know what to do. He went back to the judgment hall. He had Jesus brought to him. "Are you the king of the Jews?" he asked.

"My kingdom is not of this world," Jesus answered.

"Are you a king then?"

"You say that I am a king," Jesus said. "For this reason I came into the world—to bear witness of the truth. Every one that is of the truth hears my voice."

"What is truth?" Pilate asked. Then he went out to the Jews. "I find no fault in this man," he said.

"He stirs up the people all the way from Galilee to this place," the people shouted.

"Is he a Galilean?" Pilot asked.

"Yes," they answered.

"Galilee is under Herod's rule," he said. "Take him to Herod."

Herod did not live in Jerusalem, but he was visiting Jerusalem for the Passover. He was glad when Jesus was brought to him. He had heard about Jesus and wanted to see a miracle. He questioned Jesus himself. But Jesus would not answer.

Herod could find nothing wrong with Jesus either. But he wanted to please the Jewish leaders. So he made fun of Jesus and mocked him. Then he sent Jesus back to Pilate.

As Pilate sat on the judgment seat, he was given a note. It was from his wife. It said, "Have nothing to do with this just man. I have suffered many things in a dream because of him."

It was the custom that during the Feast of the Passover the governor would free one prisoner. Pilate knew that the Jewish leaders were jealous of Jesus. He knew that was why they wanted him to die. He hoped that if he offered to free Jesus, the people would accept.

"Should I free Jesus, the king of the Jews?" Pilate asked the multitude.

But the Jewish leaders told the people to ask for Barabbas. Barabbas was in prison for rebellion and murder. So when Pilate asked, "Whom shall I free?" the crowd cried, "Barabbas! Barabbas!"

"Then what shall I do with Jesus?"

"Crucify him. Crucify him!" the people shouted at once.

"Why? What evil has he done?" Pilate asked.

But they only cried louder, "Crucify him! Crucify him!"

When Pilate saw that he could not change their minds, he took water and washed his hands. "I am innocent of the blood of this just person," he said.

"His blood come upon us and our children," the multitude cried.

So Pilate released Barabbas to the people and ordered that Jesus be scourged. This was done with a whip that had three thongs. Braided into each thong were pieces of metal and glass.

After the scourging, they took Jesus to a hall called Praetorium. There the soldiers took away his clothes and put a purple robe over his shoulders. Then they placed a reed in his hands. They pretended it was a king's scepter. Finally they made a crown of thorns which they pushed onto his head.

Laughing and mocking, they bowed. "Hail, King of the Jews!" they said. Then they spit upon Jesus and hit him on the head with the reed.

After this Pilate again stood before the people. He brought Jesus out wearing the crown of thorns and the purple robe. "Behold the man!" he said.

But the crowd did not feel sorry for the beaten man. Instead they shouted again, "Crucify him! Crucify him!"

"But I find no fault in him," Pilate said.

"We have a law," the priests said. "He ought to die because he made himself the Son of God."

These words frightened Pilate. He asked Jesus, "What are you?" Jesus did not answer.

"Do you not speak to me?" Pilate asked. "Do you not know that I have power to crucify you or to free you?"

"You could have no power against me except it were given you from above," Jesus said.

Once more Pilate sought to free Jesus, but the people said, "If you let this man go, you are not Caesar's friend." Then they began to chant, "Crucify him! Crucify him!"

"Shall I crucify your king?" Pilate asked.

"We have no king but Caesar," the chief priest answered. So Pilate gave Jesus to them to be crucified.

—

MATTHEW 26–27; MARK 14–15;
LUKE 22–23; JOHN 18

The soldiers put the cross on Jesus' back and marched him through the streets. But Jesus was tired and hungry. The terrible beating had made him weak. The cross was too heavy. He stumbled and fell to the ground.

Seeing that he could not carry the cross, the soldiers pulled a man from the crowd. His name was Simon of Cyrene. They lifted the cross from Jesus and put it on Simon. Then they continued through the city and out the gate. Soon they came to a hill called Calvary. The hill was also called Golgotha. Both words mean "place of the skull."

At the top of the hill, the soldiers gave Jesus vinegar mixed with gall. But when Jesus tasted it, he would not drink it. Then they nailed his hands and wrists and feet to the cross and lifted it up.

Jesus knew the soldiers were only following orders. "Father, forgive them," he said, "for they know not what they do."

Pilate had ordered that a title be placed on Jesus' cross. The sign said in three languages, "This is Jesus of Nazareth the king of the Jews." When the Jews saw the sign, they were angry. "Write not 'the king of the Jews,'" they said. "Write, 'This is he that said I am Jesus, the king of the Jews.'"

But Pilate said, "What I have written, I have written. Let it alone."

Now it was the custom for the soldiers to keep the clothing of people who were crucified. Jesus had a fine cloak. It was woven in one piece and had no seam. It was worth a lot of money. All of the soldiers wanted it. To decide who would get it, they knelt below the cross and cast lots.

Around the cross the people mocked. "He saved others! Himself he cannot save!" they cried. "If he is the king of Israel, let him come down from the cross. Then we will believe him."

One of the thieves who was being crucified near Jesus joined in. "If you are Christ, save yourself and us," he cried.

But the other thief said, "Do you not fear God? We are getting what we deserve. But this man has done nothing wrong." Then he said to Jesus, "Lord, remember me when you come into your kingdom."

Jesus answered him, "Verily, I say unto you, today you shall be with me in paradise."

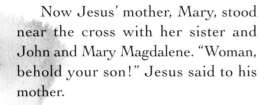

Now Jesus' mother, Mary, stood near the cross with her sister and John and Mary Magdalene. "Woman, behold your son!" Jesus said to his mother.

Then he said to John, "Behold your mother!" From that hour John took Mary into his own home and cared for her.

Jesus hung on the cross for hours. Then suddenly the sun was hidden. After three hours of darkness, Jesus cried with a loud voice, "My God, my God, why have you forsaken me?"

Jesus then said, "I thirst."

Someone filled a sponge with vinegar and gall. Others shouted, "Leave him alone. Let us see whether Elias will come to take him down." But the man put the sponge on the end of a reed and lifted it up to Jesus' mouth, so he could drink.

After Jesus sipped the vinegar, he cried with a loud voice, "Father, into your hands I commend my spirit!" Then, bowing his head, he died.

At that same moment, the veil of the temple ripped into two pieces. The earth quaked, and rocks broke apart. The soldiers were frightened. They said, "Truly this was the Son of God."

By now it was almost the Sabbath. The soldiers, in order to make the thieves die faster, broke their legs. But when they came to Jesus, he was already dead. So they thrust a spear into his side, and water and blood poured from the wound.

A rich man named Joseph of Arimathea went to Pilate. He asked if he could lay the body of Jesus in his tomb. Pilate agreed. So Joseph and a friend prepared the body. First they anointed it with myrrh and aloes. Then they wrapped it in fine linen. They laid the body of Jesus in Joseph's tomb. Then they rolled a great stone over the door and left.

The next day, the chief priests and Pharisees went to Pilate. They said, "Sir, when Jesus was alive, he said, 'After three days I will rise again.' Therefore, put guards at the grave until the third day. If you do not, his disciples might come by night, steal his body away, and say that he is risen."

Pilate answered, "You may have soldiers. Go your way and make the grave as secure as you can."

And so a guard was placed so that no one could steal Jesus' body.

—

MATTHEW 27;
MARK 15;
LUKE 23; JOHN 19

JESUS LIVES AGAIN

Early Sunday morning, a great earthquake shook the ground. Two angels came down from heaven. They rolled back the stone from the door of the tomb and sat on it. The angels' faces were like lightning, and their clothing was as white as snow. The soldiers guarding the tomb were so frightened they fell to the earth as if they were dead.

Mary Magdalene knew nothing of all this. She arose early that morning and prepared sweet spices. Before the sun was up, she hurried to the tomb, hoping to anoint Jesus' body with the spices. But when she arrived, the tomb was open, and two angels were sitting on the stone.

Mary was amazed. She ran to find Peter and John. "They have taken the Lord out of the tomb," she told them. "We know not where they have laid him."

Peter and John ran to the tomb. John got there first, stooped to look inside, and saw the linen clothes lying where the body had been. Soon Peter arrived and entered the tomb. He saw the linen clothes. He also saw the napkin that had covered Jesus' head. It was folded and lying in a different place.

Amazed and in awe, the apostles left. But Mary Magdalene stayed there weeping. After awhile she looked into the tomb once more. This time she saw two angels. One sat where Jesus' head had been and the other where his feet had been.

The angels asked, "Woman, why do you weep?"

Mary answered, "Because they have taken away my Lord, and I know not where they have laid him." Then, turning back to the garden, she saw a man.

The man asked her, "Woman, why do you weep? Whom do you seek?"

Mary thought the man was the gardener. She said, "Sir, if you have taken Jesus away, tell me where you have laid him."

The man said, "Mary."

At the sound of her name, Mary turned back. It was Jesus!

"Rabboni!" she cried.

Jesus said to her, "Hold me not, for I have not yet ascended to my Father. But go to my brethren. Say to them that I ascend unto my Father, and your Father, and to my God, and your God."

Mary obeyed. She hurried to tell the apostles that Jesus was alive and that she had seen him. But they did not believe her.

Now other women also went to the tomb with spices for the body. When they saw the open grave and the angels, they were afraid.

The angels said, "Be not afraid. You seek Jesus of Nazareth, who was crucified. But why do you seek the living among the dead? He is risen. He is not here. Remember what he told you in Galilee: 'The Son of Man must be delivered into the hands of sinful men, be crucified, and on the third day rise again.'"

The women looked inside the tomb. Just as the angels said, the body was not there.

The angels said, "Go your way. Tell his disciples and Peter."

The women hurried to tell the apostles all they had seen and heard. But as they went, Jesus appeared to them.

"Be not afraid," he told them. "Tell my brethren to go into Galilee. There they shall see me."

The women found the apostles and told them all they had seen. But the words seemed like idle tales to the apostles.

Later that day, two of the disciples were traveling to the village of Emmaus. As they walked and talked about the things that had happened, Jesus joined them. But they did not recognize Jesus.

"What are you speaking of?" Jesus asked them. "And why are you so sad?"

One of the disciples, Cleopas, answered,

"Are you a stranger in Jerusalem? Have you not heard the things that have happened?"

Jesus asked, "What things?"

The disciples said, "About Jesus of Nazareth. He was a prophet mighty in deed and word." Then they told the story of Jesus' crucifixion. When the story was over, they added, "We thought he would save Israel."

Jesus said to them, "O fools, and slow of heart to believe all that the prophets have spoken. Ought Christ not to have suffered these things, and to enter into his glory?" Then Jesus recited the scriptures that explained his mission on earth.

As they drew near to Emmaus, the disciples stopped. "Stay with us," they said, "for it is almost evening." And so he stayed.

They ate supper, and he took bread and blessed it. Then he broke it and gave it to them. As they ate, their eyes were opened. Suddenly they knew it was Jesus. But as soon as they knew him, he vanished from their sight.

Quickly the two apostles returned to Jerusalem. They found all the apostles except for Thomas meeting together. They told them everything that had happened. As they spoke, Jesus suddenly appeared in the middle of the room. "Peace be unto you," he said.

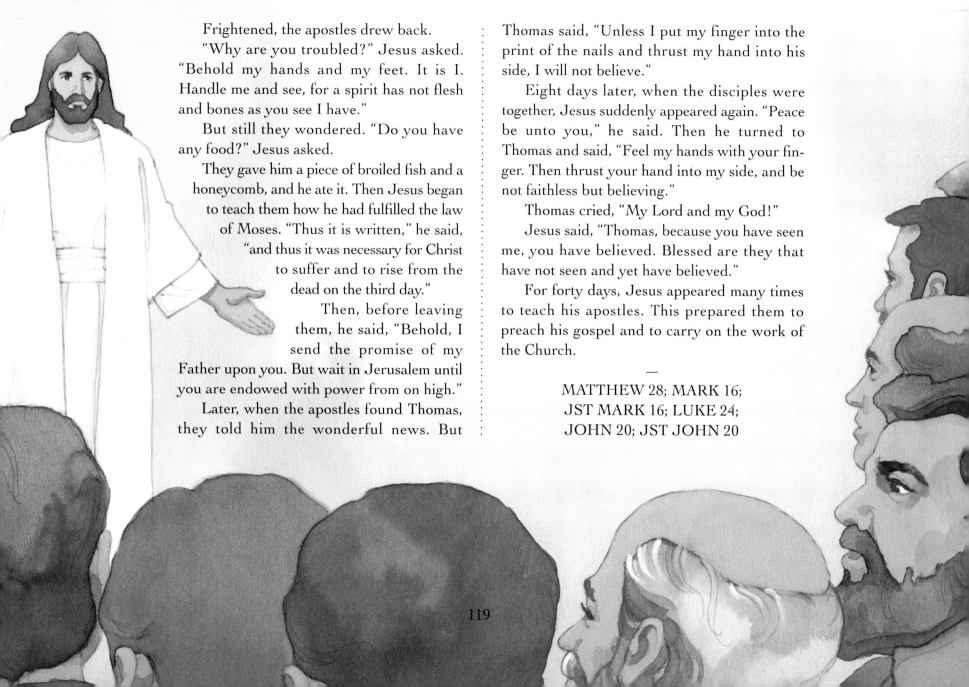

Frightened, the apostles drew back.

"Why are you troubled?" Jesus asked. "Behold my hands and my feet. It is I. Handle me and see, for a spirit has not flesh and bones as you see I have."

But still they wondered. "Do you have any food?" Jesus asked.

They gave him a piece of broiled fish and a honeycomb, and he ate it. Then Jesus began to teach them how he had fulfilled the law of Moses. "Thus it is written," he said, "and thus it was necessary for Christ to suffer and to rise from the dead on the third day."

Then, before leaving them, he said, "Behold, I send the promise of my Father upon you. But wait in Jerusalem until you are endowed with power from on high."

Later, when the apostles found Thomas, they told him the wonderful news. But Thomas said, "Unless I put my finger into the print of the nails and thrust my hand into his side, I will not believe."

Eight days later, when the disciples were together, Jesus suddenly appeared again. "Peace be unto you," he said. Then he turned to Thomas and said, "Feel my hands with your finger. Then thrust your hand into my side, and be not faithless but believing."

Thomas cried, "My Lord and my God!"

Jesus said, "Thomas, because you have seen me, you have believed. Blessed are they that have not seen and yet have believed."

For forty days, Jesus appeared many times to teach his apostles. This prepared them to preach his gospel and to carry on the work of the Church.

—

MATTHEW 28; MARK 16; JST MARK 16; LUKE 24; JOHN 20; JST JOHN 20

Fifty days after Passover, the Jews held another feast called Pentecost. To celebrate Pentecost, the apostles and other disciples gathered in one place. As they visited, a sound from heaven filled the house. The sound was like a mighty, rushing wind. But there was no wind! Then suddenly flames of fire rested above each of them, and they were filled with the Holy Ghost. Prompted by the Spirit, they all began to speak in tongues.

At that time there were men from every nation dwelling in Jerusalem. As the news spread through the city, people hurried to see. As they gathered, the disciples taught them in their own language.

"Are these men not Galileans?" the people asked. "How do we hear in our own language?"

Amazed, they asked, "What does this mean?"

"They are full of new wine!" some exclaimed and started to leave.

But Peter lifted up his voice and said, "Listen to my words. These men are not drunk. This is what the prophet Joel spoke of. He said that in the last days God would pour out his Spirit upon all flesh." Then Peter taught the people about the Savior and asked them to be baptized. That day three thousand people were baptized.

From then on, the Day of Pentecost was known as the day when the gift of the Holy Ghost was given to the apostles.

—

ACTS 2; JST ACTS 2

120

After the Savior's death, Peter became the head of the Church.

One day, Peter and John were on their way to the temple. They passed a lame man. He asked for alms.

Peter stopped. "Look on us," he said.

The man looked at Peter. He thought Peter would give him money. But instead, Peter said, "I have no silver or gold. But what I have I give you. In the name of Jesus Christ of Nazareth, rise up and walk."

Peter took the man by the right hand and lifted him to his feet. Suddenly his ankles were strong. He began to leap and dance with joy. Excited and grateful, he walked into the temple with Peter and John. All who saw this were amazed. They, too, praised God and wondered at the miracle.

Peter said to the people, "You men of Israel, why do you marvel at this? Why do you look on us, as though by our own power or holiness we had made this man to walk? Faith in Jesus Christ has made this man strong."

Peter continued, "Repent, therefore, and be converted, that your sins may be blotted out."

As Peter taught the people, the priests, Sadducees, and captain of the temple became very upset. Peter was preaching the teachings of Jesus. They could not let such doctrines continue to spread! They wanted to destroy the followers of Christ. So they put Peter and John in prison.

The next morning Peter, John, and the man who was healed were brought before Caiaphas and other Jewish rulers. The rulers asked, "By what power did you perform this miracle?"

Peter was filled with the Holy Ghost. He said, "You crucified Jesus but God raised him from the dead. It is through the name of Jesus Christ that this man stands before you whole."

When the rulers saw the boldness of Peter and John, they marveled. These were unlearned men. How dare they speak and act like that?

After the prisoners were taken away, the leaders talked together. They said, "What shall we do to these men? They have done a miracle. We cannot deny it. But let us threaten them so that no one else will learn of this thing."

So they had Peter and John brought back. They said to Peter and John, "Do not preach or teach anymore in the name of Jesus!"

But Peter and John answered, "Is it right to obey you or to obey God? You judge. We must speak the things which we have seen and heard."

The priests tried long and hard, but they could think of nothing to accuse Peter and John of doing. Reluctantly, they let them go. Peter and John went back to the other apostles and told them what had happened.

When the rulers discovered that Peter and John were still preaching, they became angry. They cast them into prison again. But an angel of the Lord came during the night, opened the doors, and led them out of the prison. The angel said, "Go, stand and teach in the temple."

Early the next morning, Peter and John went to the temple and began to teach. The chief priests did not know they had escaped from the prison. They asked for the prisoners to be brought before them. The soldiers returned shortly. They reported, "The prison is safely shut. The guards are at their posts. But the prisoners are gone."

Just then a messenger arrived. He said, "The men you put in prison are standing in the temple teaching the people."

The priests sent soldiers to the temple. They brought Peter and John back.

"Didn't we command you not to teach in this name?" the priests said. "You have filled Jerusalem with his doctrine. You intend to bring this man's blood upon us!"

Peter and John answered, "We ought to obey God rather than men. The God of our fathers raised up Jesus, whom you slew."

When the priests heard this, they were cut to the heart. They talked together about how they could kill Peter and John. But one of them, a Pharisee named Gamaliel, stepped forward. He said, "Let these men alone. If this work is of men, it will come to nothing. If it is of God, you cannot overthrow it."

The priests decided not to kill the apostles. Instead, they gave orders for them to be beaten. After the beating, the priests said, "You may go. But you are not to teach among this people again!"

Peter and John left quickly. But they were not sorrowful. They left rejoicing because they considered it a great privilege to suffer for Jesus' name. After that, they continued to teach the people about Jesus Christ. Thousands were baptized. Soon other men were called to help preach and teach the gospel.

Now, up until this time, the gospel had been taught only to the Jews. But one day when Peter was praying on a housetop in the town of Joppa, he saw a vision. In the vision, he saw the heavens open and a great sheet come down to the earth. The sheet was tied at the four corners and was holding wild beasts, birds, and creeping things. Each of these creatures had one thing in common. Each was unclean under the law of Moses. As Peter looked at the animals, a voice said, "Rise, Peter. Kill and eat."

Peter answered, "Not so, Lord! I have never eaten any thing that is common or unclean."

The voice said, "What God has cleansed, call not common."

This message and Peter's answer were repeated three times. Then the sheet was taken into heaven again.

While Peter wondered about the vision and what it meant, messengers came to his house. The Spirit said to him, "Three men seek you. Go with them. Doubt nothing, for I have sent them."

So Peter met the messengers. They told him a Roman soldier named Cornelius sent them to find a man named Peter. Peter said, "I am the one you seek. What do you want?"

The messengers said, "Cornelius is a just man. A holy angel from God told him to send for you and to hear your words."

The next day, Peter went with the men to Caesarea. Cornelius was waiting for him. When he saw Peter, he fell down on the ground to worship him. Peter said, "Stand up. I myself am also a man."

Then Peter entered the house. Cornelius had gathered his relatives and friends to meet Peter. Peter greeted them. He said, "You know that it is unlawful for a Jew to keep company with men of other nations. But God has shown me that I should not call any man common or unclean. Therefore, why have you sent for me?"

Cornelius replied, "Four days ago, I was fasting. At the ninth hour I prayed, and a man stood before me in bright clothing. He said, 'Cornelius, God hears your prayers and remembers the alms you have given. Send to Joppa, for Peter.' So I sent for you. Therefore, we are here to hear all things that God has commanded you to say."

Peter said, "Truly, I see that God is no

PETER

respecter of persons. In every nation, he that works righteousness is accepted of God." And he began to teach the people about Jesus Christ. When he had finished, they wanted to be baptized.

During the next year, Peter and the apostles continued to teach. Hundreds and thousands of people believed and joined the Church. But the persecution against the Church also grew. James, the brother of John, was killed with a sword. Then Herod began to persecute the Christians. When Herod saw how much this pleased the Jewish leaders, he had Peter thrown into prison. Herod assigned four squads of four soldiers to guard Peter. When the Church members heard that Peter was in prison, they prayed for him.

One night, Peter was sleeping between two guards. He was bound with chains. Two more guards were at the door keeping watch. Suddenly a light shone in the room. It was an angel. The angel said, "Get up quickly."

As Peter stood, the chains fell off his hands. "Now get dressed and put on your sandals," the angel said.

When Peter was dressed, the angel said, "Put on your cloak and follow me." So Peter followed, not knowing if he was fleeing the prison or if he was seeing a vision. They passed the first guard and the second. As they neared the iron gate that led into the city, it opened by itself, and they went out to the street. As soon as they were safely out of the prison, the angel left.

"Now I know this is no vision," Peter said. "The Lord has sent his angel to deliver me." Then he hurried to the house of Mary, the mother of John, where many of the members of the Church were together praying.

When Peter arrived, he knocked at the door of the gate. A woman named Rhoda answered. When she heard Peter's voice she became so excited that she ran back inside.

"Peter has come!" she cried.

"You are crazy!" they answered.

"I know it is he!" Rhoda insisted.

"Surely it must be his angel!" they said.

But Peter kept knocking, and when they finally opened the door they were surprised. When he was safe inside, Peter told them all that had happened. He told them to tell the other apostles. Then he left to continue the work of the Lord.

—

ACTS 3–5, 10–12

124

Saul was a Pharisee. He led the persecution of the Christians. He raided homes in Judea and Samaria, hunting and capturing Christians.

But Saul was not content to fight against the Church in Judea only. One day he was traveling on the road to Damascus to persecute the Christians there. As he was traveling, a bright light overpowered him, and he fell to the ground.

"Saul, Saul, why do you persecute me?" a voice asked.

Saul asked, "Who are you, Lord?"

The voice said, "I am Jesus, whom you persecute."

"Lord, what do you want me to do?" Saul asked.

Jesus said, "Go into the city, and it shall be told you what you must do."

The men who journeyed with Saul heard a voice but could see nothing. They waited silently while Saul spoke. Finally Saul arose, but he could not see. The men who were with him led him on to Damascus. He stayed for three days, eating and drinking nothing.

125

During this same time, a Christian named Ananias had a vision. In this vision the Lord said to Ananias, "Go to the street which is called Straight. Ask at the house of Judas for a man called Saul of Tarsus. He has seen in a vision a man named Ananias blessing him and giving back his sight."

Ananias said, "Lord, I have heard much of this man. I have heard of the evil he has done to your Saints in Jerusalem."

But the Lord said unto Ananias, "Go on your way. I have chosen him. He will bear my name before Gentiles, kings, and the children of Israel. I will show him the great things he must suffer for my name's sake."

So Ananias went his way, entered the house, and laid his hands on Saul. Ananias prayed, saying, "Brother Saul, the Lord, even Jesus that appeared to you, has sent me. He sent me that you might receive your sight and be filled with the Holy Ghost."

At that moment scales fell from Saul's eyes. He could see. Joyously he arose and was baptized. Then he ate and was strengthened.

Saul stayed in Damascus for many days, learning from the disciples. Soon he began to preach in the synagogues. He testified to anyone who would listen that Jesus was the Son of God.

The people asked, "Is this not the man who destroyed those who called on Christ's name in Jerusalem?" But Saul continued to teach and preach the gospel.

When the rulers heard this, they tried to find a way to kill Saul. But Saul knew of their plans. The disciples helped him escape by letting him down from the city wall in a basket. He fled to Jerusalem. In Jerusalem, he found the disciples, but they were afraid of him. They did not know he had been converted to Jesus' church.

A man named Barnabas knew of Saul's conversion and good works. He took Saul to the apostles. There Saul testified that he had seen the Lord and been baptized. He told the apostles how he had preached in Damascus. He said he wanted to teach with them in Jerusalem. The apostles listened carefully and felt the truth of Saul's words. They knew he had been sent by Jesus. They invited him to stay with them and to help in the work. After that, Saul used his Roman name, Paul. And he preached with great boldness in the name of Jesus Christ.

—

ACTS 8–9

For many years Paul traveled and preached the gospel. He healed many people and performed many miracles. But he was stoned, imprisoned, and often persecuted for his faith in Jesus Christ.

Once in Jerusalem a mob tried to kill him. Roman soldiers took him from the mob and kept him in the prison to protect him. While Paul was in the prison, the Lord appeared to him. "Be of good cheer," the Lord said. "For as you have testified of me in Jerusalem, so must you bear witness at Rome."

The next day, certain of the Jews swore that they would not eat or drink till they had killed Paul. But the son of Paul's sister heard of their plan, and he told the chief captain of the Roman soldiers. The chief captain sent two hundred soldiers, seventy horsemen, and two hundred spearmen to take Paul to Felix, the Roman governor in Caesarea.

After he arrived in Caesarea, Paul was put in prison. The Jews told the Romans that Paul was plotting to rebel against them. Paul was brought to trial. During his trial, Paul preached the gospel to Felix and the others who were there.

Felix kept Paul prisoner for two years. After two years, a new ruler named Festus decided to give Paul to the Jews to be tried. Paul knew that such a trial would not be fair. He said, "But I am a citizen of Rome." By Roman law, that meant they had to send him to Rome to be tried. There he could explain his case to Caesar and let Caesar decide if he was innocent or guilty.

The Romans put Paul on a ship going to Italy. The ship sailed for many days. Finally, the sailors stopped at the island of Crete. Winter was coming, and the sea was getting too dangerous for sailing. But the captain of the ship was impatient. He wanted to sail on anyway.

Paul warned the soldiers who were guarding him. "Sirs," he said, "I see that this voyage will end with much damage, not only to the ship, but also to our lives."

But the centurion in charge of the soldiers would not listen to Paul or the other soldiers. He agreed with the captain to sail on. So they set out again. Soon the south wind began to blow,

and the sailors lost their way. Fierce winds and great waves tossed the ship. The sailors tried everything to save the ship. But nothing helped.

The passengers were terrified. Paul said to them, "Sirs, you should have listened to me and not left Crete. But now I tell you to be of good cheer. No one will lose his life. Only the ship will be lost. This night an angel told me, 'Fear not, Paul. You must be brought before Caesar. God will keep everyone who sails with you safe.'"

Fourteen days later, the storm still raged. The ship was in shallow waters. The crew saw the danger. They began to take down the lifeboats so they could abandon the ship. But Paul said to the centurion, "Unless they stay in the ship, you cannot be saved."

This time the centurion believed Paul. He cut the ropes of the lifeboats to keep the sailors

from escaping. Paul then told the 216 passengers they should eat, because they would need their strength. He told them again that they would not lose their lives.

After they ate, daylight came. Once more the crew tried to sail. But the winds were too strong and the waves too violent. The ship ran aground, and the waves broke it apart.

As the ship began to sink, the soldiers were afraid they would be punished if they lost the prisoners. So they decided to kill the prisoners. But the centurion wanted to save Paul. He ordered all the prisoners to jump into the sea and swim to shore. Grabbing boards and pieces of the ship, the prisoners all made it safely to the island of Melita.

People on the island saw what was happening. They helped rescue the passengers. They built a fire and brought food and clothing and cared for the injured. Paul also helped. He gathered sticks and laid them on the fire. As he did so, a poisonous snake called a viper came out of the heat and wound itself on his hand. The people of Melita saw the viper and said among themselves, "This man must be a murderer. He may have escaped the sea, but vengeance will not let him live."

But Paul shook the viper into the fire and felt no harm. The people watched Paul intently. They expected to see him swell up and fall dead. They waited and waited, but nothing happened. They were so astonished they began to whisper among themselves that Paul must be a god.

Paul and the other prisoners stayed in Melita for three months. Finally, another ship came and took them to Rome.

Paul lived in a house in Rome for two years. Even though he was still a prisoner, the Romans let him have visitors. He taught all who came to him about the Lord Jesus Christ. He even called the Jewish leaders together and tried to teach them the gospel, but they would not listen.

Eventually Paul was released. After that he was arrested and put in prison several more times. Finally he was killed. But Paul had done what the Lord commanded him to do, and so he was at peace. In one of his last letters he wrote, "I am ready to be offered. The time for me to leave this life is near. I have fought a good fight, I have finished my course, I have kept the faith."

Indeed, Paul not only kept the faith, but he gave that faith to many others.

—

ACTS 23–28; 2 TIMOTHY 4:6–7

Abram—The father of Isaac and grandfather of Jacob and Esau was first named Abram. The Lord changed Abram's name to Abraham. Abram means "exalted father." Abraham means "father of a multitude."

Amalekites—Amalek was the son of Eliphaz and the grandson of Esau. His descendants became known as Amalekites. The Amalekites warred against the Hebrews from the time of Moses until the time of Saul and David.

Apostle—Jesus chose twelve of his disciples to be special witnesses of him. These twelve were called apostles.

Ark of the Covenant—God commanded Moses to have the children of Israel make a box or chest. This chest was used to carry the scriptures and other sacred things such as a pot of manna and Aaron's rod. The box was known as the Ark of the Covenant. Sometimes it was also called the "Ark of the Lord," "Ark of God," "Ark of Jehovah," or "Ark of the Testimony." It was a rectangular box made of acacia wood covered in gold. It was 2½ cubits long, 1½ cubits wide, and 1½ cubits high. When the children of Israel traveled, it was carried on poles inserted in rings at the four lower corners. The lid was called the Mercy Seat and held two cherubim facing each other. The ark was a symbol of the divine presence that led the people.

Ashes—See "Sackcloth and ashes."

Baal—Baal was one of the false gods worshipped by people in Phoenicia, Moab, and other places.

Beatitudes—When Jesus gave the Sermon on the Mount, he told the people of certain traits that would bring them blessings. For example, those who hunger and thirst after righteousness will be blessed with the Holy Ghost (see JST Matthew 5:6). These descriptions are called the Beatitudes. The word *beatitude* means "supreme blessedness or happiness."

Betrothed—The first of the legal steps to marry someone was called a betrothal. When a man and woman had taken this step they were said to be betrothed.

Calvary—The place where Jesus was crucified was called *calvaria* in Latin. *Calvary* is the English form of the Latin word. It means "a skull."

Champion—In biblical times a champion would sometimes be chosen by an army to fight the champion of an opposing army. The winner of this contest determined which army won the battle. Goliath was the champion of the Philistine army. David volunteered to be the champion of the Hebrew army.

Charger—A large, shallow dish is called a charger.

Cherubim—*Cherubim* is another word for angels. Two figures called cherubim faced each other on the Mercy Seat of the Ark of the Covenant. These were symbolic figures, representing guardians, whose wings protected the altar. If there is only one angel, it is called a cherub.

Christ—*Christ* is a Greek word meaning "the anointed one."

Clean—In biblical times, things that were forbidden such as certain foods or acts were called unclean, and the foods or acts that were allowed were called clean. The blood and fat of animals were unclean, as were certain types of meat. Unclean foods could not be eaten by the Israelites. Touching a dead body or entering the home of a Gentile were considered unclean acts. Anyone who did these things would need to "repent" and go through a process that would make him or her clean again. This was part of the old law that was done away with when Jesus was resurrected.

Cubit—A cubit was a measurement of distance for the Hebrews. It was the distance from the elbow to the tip of the fingers. It was about 18 inches or 45 centimeters.

Disciple—A follower of Jesus.

Feasts—The law of Moses commanded that three times a year all the males of the covenant should come before the Lord. The three times were the Feast of Unleavened Bread, the Feast of Weeks, and the Feast of Tabernacles.

Gall—*Gall* is a word used for anything bitter. Sometimes the herb wormwood or the gum resin myrrh are called gall.

Golgotha—In the Aramaic language, the name of the place where Christ was crucified is Golgotha. Golgotha means "skull."

Hebrews—The descendants of Abraham were called the Hebrews. Sometimes they are also called the children of Israel.

Horn—To people in biblical times, a horn was a symbol of power. This was because an animal used its horns to fight its enemies and display its power. Therefore, when Hannah sings her praises to the Lord and says, "Exalt the horn of his anointed" (1 Samuel 2:10), she is praying that the power of the anointed will be great.

Israel—The Lord changed Jacob's name to Israel, which means "one who prevails with God."

Jews—The people who lived in the land of Judah became known as Jews.

Leaven — The ingredient in bread (often yeast) that makes it rise is called leaven. But leaven makes dough rise by fermenting, so it is sometimes a symbol of things that corrupt.

Leprosy — In hot climates in biblical times, leprosy was a common disease that caused ulcers of the skin and led to a loss of feeling, paralysis, other infections, and deformity.

Messiah — *Messiah* is a Hebrew word meaning "the anointed one."

Midianites — One of Abraham's sons from his wife Keturah was named Midian. Midian's descendants became a wandering group of people called the Midianites. They were often at war with the children of Israel.

Miriam — The sister who watched out for Moses while he was in the ark hidden in the bulrushes was Miriam. Miriam means "exalted."

Moabites — Lot's daughter had a son named Moab. His descendants are called the Moabites; they were constantly at war with the Hebrews.

Mount Moriah — Abraham climbed Mount Moriah with his son Isaac to offer Isaac as a sacrifice. Later Solomon's temple was built on Mount Moriah.

Myrrh — One of the gifts the wise men brought to the infant Jesus was a sweet-smelling gum called myrrh. It was very valuable and was used as incense, as perfume, for embalming, and in the purification ceremony for women. The myrrh plant is covered with long spikelike thorns.

Nazarite — Men or women who dedicated themselves to the Lord were called Nazarites. They followed certain rules that set them apart from other people; they did not drink strong drink and they never cut their hair (see Numbers 6). In the story of Samson we are told that a "razor never came upon his head," which meant he was a Nazarite. Sometimes a parent would dedicate a child to be a Nazarite.

Parable — Jesus often told stories in order to teach people. These stories are called parables.

Passover — Once a year the children of Israel held a Feast of the Passover. This was to remind them of the time in Egypt when the Lord killed the firstborn of every Egyptian household. But he "passed over" the houses of the Israelites and did not slay their children.

Philistines — The Philistines were a warlike people who migrated from the Aegean basin to the southern coast of Palestine. They came in the early twelfth century B.C. They were some of the main rivals of the children of Israel.

Pottage — A soup or stew made with lentils or herbs, and sometimes with meat, is called pottage.

Prophet—A prophet is a man who knows by personal revelation from the Holy Ghost that Jesus is the Son of God. Moses said he wished all his people were prophets (see Numbers 11:29). The man who leads the Church is always a prophet, seer, and revelator.

Prophetess—A prophetess is a woman who knows by personal revelation from the Holy Ghost that Jesus is the Son of God.

Ransom—When Jesus paid the price for our sins, he ransomed us. This means he suffered the consequences of our sin. Then, if we repent, we will be redeemed from the consequences.

Reign of the Judges—After Joshua and until Saul, during a period of about 200 years, judges ruled the children of Israel. This time was called the Reign of the Judges. Gideon and Deborah were two of these judges.

Rent Clothes—*Rent* is the past tense of the verb *to rend*. To rend something is to tear it. In Bible times, when people were full of sorrow they would rend their clothing as a symbol that their hearts were broken.

Ruth—Ruth was a Moabite woman who was converted to the gospel and moved to Israel. She married Boaz, and their great-grandson David became king of Israel.

Sackcloth and ashes—A dark-colored material made of goat or camel hair was used for making grain bags and garments. This material was called sackcloth and was very uncomfortable to wear. When people were sorrowful or repentant, they would wear sackcloth and put ashes upon their bodies as a symbol of their distress.

Sarah—Abraham's first wife was Sarai. When the Lord changed Abram's name to Abraham, he also changed Sarai's name to Sarah. Sarah means "princess."

Savior—A savior is a person who saves someone else by doing something for them that they cannot do for themselves. Through the Atonement, Jesus Christ saved us from sin and eternal death, and thus he is the Savior of us all.

Seed—In biblical times a person's children, grandchildren, and other descendants were called his or her seed.

Sheaf—A bundle of cut stalks of grain or similar plants that was bound with straw or twine was called a sheaf.

Shiloh—Shiloh was the sacred city and center of government for the Israelites from the time they settled in Palestine until the Reign of the Judges was almost ended. The tabernacle was in Shiloh.

Sop—A piece of food dipped in liquid is called a sop.

Spoils—Goods or property seized unlawfully, especially in wartime, are called spoils.

Suffer—In biblical times the word *suffer* meant to permit or to allow.

Timbrel—A hand-held percussion instrument used to accompany religious hymns was called a timbrel. It was something like a tambourine.

Tongues—Sometimes the Spirit helps people speak in a language they have not learned. This is called speaking in tongues or the gift of tongues.

Translated—From the time of Adam until the time of Melchizedek, it was not uncommon for faithful members of the Church to be translated. This means they were taken into heaven without dying. In heaven they performed special missions until it was time for them to be resurrected. Moses, Elijah, and John the Beloved were some of the prophets who were translated.

Unclean—See "Clean."

Virgin—A pure or chaste woman who is not married is a virgin.

Zion—Zion is the name given by the Lord to his Saints. It means "the pure in heart." It is also a name given to the place where the pure in heart live.